CONTENTS

FOREWORD 7

I

INTRODUCTION 9
a) General Economic Background 9
b) Fiscal Policy 13
c) Financing by Sector 14
d) Financial Institutions and Markets 19

II

INSTRUMENTS OF MONETARY POLICY AND OPERATING TARGETS 35
a) Instruments of Monetary Policy 35
b) Main Operating Targets 39
c) Actions on Bank Liquidity 41

III

THE USE OF MONETARY POLICY AND ITS IMPACT ON FINANCIAL VARIABLES 43
a) The Dating of Policy Phases and their Cyclical Context 43
b) The Problem of Capital Flows: Some General Experience from Policy Phases. 57
c) The Impact of Monetary Policy on Domestic Financial Variables 66

IV

THE IMPACT ON DEMAND AND ULTIMATE POLICY OBJECTIVES 73
a) Inventories 73
b) Business Fixed Investment 77
c) Housing 84
d) Local Authority Investment 86
e) Private Consumption 86
f) Aggregate Demand, Balance of Payments and Prices 87

V

SUMMARY AND CONCLUDING REMARKS 93

Appendices

I. BANK LIQUIDITY AND THE FACTORS AFFECTING IT 101
   A. Policy Factors Affecting Bank Liquidity 101
      Minimum Reserve Requirements 101
      Rediscount Quotas 102
      Open Market Operations Affecting Bank Liquidity ... 103

3

B. Autonomous Factors Affecting Bank Liquidity 105
   External Transactions 105
   Public Sector Financing 105
   Currency in Circulation 106

II. THE COMPONENTS OF BANK LIQUIDITY AND THE FACTORS AFFECTING THEM... 107
   Domestic Money Market Assets 107
   Foreign Liquid Assets of Commercial Banks 108
   Unused Rediscount Quotas 109
   Excess Balances at the Central Bank 109
   Lombard Credits 109

III. CHRONOLOGY OF PRINCIPAL MONETARY MEASURES 113

*
* *

LIST OF TABLES AND CHARTS

TABLES

1. Structure of Demand 10
2. Balance of Payments .... 14 and 15
3. Maturity Composition of Domestic Bank Lending to the Business
   Sector .... 16 and 17
4. Sources of Housing Finance .... 16 and 17
5. Structure of Public Authorities' Indebtedness .... 20 and 21
6. Changes in Financial Assets of Households .... 22 and 23
7. Banking System: Principal Assets and Liabilities, 31st December 1971. 24 and 25
8. Dating of Policy Changes 43
9. Private Capital Movements Affecting Bank Liquidity 58
10. Special Measures Against Capital Inflows during Restrictive Policy
    Periods .... 60 and 61
11. Observed Lags from Adoption of Restrictive Monetary Policy Stance to
    Cyclical Weakening of Fixed Investment 80
Appendix I. Bundesbank Transactions in Money Market Paper with Non-
          Banks 103
          Open Market Transactions in Long-term Securities 104
Appendix II. Banks' Use of Discount and Lombard Credits 110

CHARTS

1. Trend of GNP and Prices 11
2. Trend of Current Balance of Payments 12
3. Financial Surpluses and Deficits 26
4. Credit Flows to Domestic Non-Financial Sectors, by Sector 27
5. Credit Flows to Domestic Non-Financial Sectors, by Liabilities .. 28
6. Business Sector's Gross and Net Savings and Investment 29
7. Business Sector's Borrowing 30
8. Borrowing to Finance Housebuilding 31
9. Public Sector's Borrowing 31
10. The Bond Market .... 32 and 33
11. Bank Liquidity 45
12. Bank Liquidity Developments: First Restrictive Phase 47
13. Bank Liquidity Developments: Second Restrictive Phase 49
14. Bank Liquidity Developments: Third Restrictive Phase 52
15. Bank Liquidity Developments: First Phase of Easing 54
16. Bank Liquidity Developments: Second Phase of Easing 56

17. Interest Rates and Monetary Aggregates 62
18. 3-Month Interest Arbitrage 63
19. Changes in Inventories 74
20. Equation for Inventory Investment 75
21. Non-Residential Fixed Investment 78
22. Orders for Capital Goods 79
23. Equation for Business Fixed Investment 83
24. Companies' Short-Term Debt 85
25. Housing Activity 85
26. Cyclical Development of Wages and Profits 87
27. Growth of Internal Demand 89

5

FOREWORD

This report forms part of a series of special studies on monetary policy undertaken by the Secretariat of the OECD at the request of the Economic Policy Committee. Each country has increasingly to formulate its own monetary policy within an international context. The purpose of these studies is to provide a better framework for the analysis of national monetary policies, and for international consultation regarding the use of monetary policy in Member countries for domestic demand management and balance of payments adjustment.

The need for detailed analysis on the working of monetary policy in different countries had been felt for various reasons:

i) In the recent period increased use has been made of monetary policy, and in more countries than previously, as a means of controlling demand, and as a consequence more evidence is becoming available as to the nature of its impact. It is useful to examine this evidence on an international basis and to compare the effects on demand of monetary policy in different countries.

ii) The volatility of international capital movements has increased. Though the scale of the effects to be attributed to monetary policy is difficult to quantify, the question is clearly of considerable importance for monetary authorities. Since the effects depend on the relative posture of monetary policies in different countries, they can clearly best be evaluated in the context of studies which examine the joint effects of different national monetary policies in at least the major financial countries.

The internal effects of monetary policy depend greatly on the economic and financial structure of the economy including the size of the public debt, the role of banks as financial intermediaries in the saving/investment process, the way in which housing is financed, and the scale and nature of consumer credit. These factors differ much from country to country. The external effects of monetary policy also depend to some extent on general institutional factors peculiar to different countries, and, in some cases, on the use made of policy instruments particularly designed to have external effects.

A series of country studies has, therefore, been envisaged which assembles the evidence about the working of monetary policy, taking into account differences in the economic and financial structure and the ways in which they have affected the choice of monetary instruments and the transmission process through which monetary policy has affected the financial and real sectors of the economy.

7

It has been decided to confine these studies, at least initially, to five or six countries whose monetary policies have been most important in influencing international capital movements. This report on Germany follows the study on monetary policy in Japan published in December 1972 and that on monetary policy in Italy published in May 1973. Subsequent reports will be concerned with monetary policy in France, the United States, and possibly the United Kingdom. The results of these studies will later be integrated in a general report synthesizing the separate country studies.

The present study was prepared by the Monetary Division of the Department of Economic and Statistics, with valuable assistance from other members of the Department. It was discussed at meetings of official experts from the Member countries to be covered by the studies. The report is, however, published on my sole responsibility.

Emile van LENNEP
Secretary-General

I

INTRODUCTION

This report aims at analysing the working of monetary policy in Germany, focusing on the period 1960-71, though reference is made to some important developments since 1971. The report is divided into five parts. The present introductory section reviews the general background for monetary policy in Germany as set by the main economic trends, fiscal policy and, notably, the financial structure. Part II reviews briefly the main instruments and operating targets of monetary policy, reserving a more detailed description of them for Appendix I and a chronology of their use for Appendix III. Part III is a review of policy developments in their cyclical context; it also tries to assess the impact of policy changes on capital flows, monetary and financial aggregates and interest rates. Part IV carries this evaluation further to the impact on major components of expenditures. The concluding Part V attempts an overall assessment of the use and effects of monetary policy.

a) GENERAL ECONOMIC BACKGROUND

During the period under study, the German gross national product grew on average by about 5 per cent per annum. The growth rate rose to a high level in two years of economic boom (9 per cent in 1960 and nearly 8 per cent in 1969); there was a small decline in output in 1967 (Charts 1 and 27). With the exception of the latter year, demand has been moving close to the limits set by capacity; in particular the rate of unemployment has been low. Since late 1959 the number of unemployed has stayed below 1 per cent of the total labour force, except during the 1967 recession, and the number of jobs vacant has generally been very large. Substantial recourse has been had to immigrant labour; the share of foreign workers in the total labour force rose from about 1 per cent in 1960 to 4 per cent in 1965 and about 9½ per cent in 1971.

While the overall experience has been one of high and rather smooth growth, there have been significant cyclical fluctuations in the composition of demand throughout the period (Table 1). The main factor in such shifts during the 1960's has been uneven increases in exports: they came about mainly during three strong export booms—in 1959-60, 1963 and 1968-69 (Chart 2). In these three cases the export booms triggered off, with a short time lag, an upsurge in domestic demand, notably business fixed investment; the years 1960, 1964-65 and 1968-69 were all clear examples of this process. The exports and investment booms in turn tended to generate subsequent above-average increases in private consumption.

9

Table 1. STRUCTURE OF DEMAND
PERCENTAGE SHARE IN GNP AT CURRENT PRICES

	Private consumption	Public consumption	Gross fixed investment				Stock building	Exports	Imports	External balance
			Total	Public	Residential	Other private				
1959	58.0	13.4	23.6	3.1	6.2	14.3	1.5	23.6	20.1	3.6
1960	57.0	13.6	24.2	3.1	5.7	15.4	2.9	20.7	18.3	2.4
1961	56.8	13.9	25.3	3.4	5.8	16.1	2.0	19.6	17.6	2.0
1962	57.0	14.8	26.0	3.9	6.0	16.1	1.1	19.0	18.0	1.0
1963	56.8	15.5	25.8	4.2	6.0	15.6	0.5	19.4	18.1	1.3
1959-63[1]	57.1	14.2	24.9	3.5	5.9	15.5	1.6	20.5	18.4	1.2
1964	55.8	14.8	27.0	4.6	6.4	16.0	1.2	19.7	18.5	1.2
1965	56.2	15.2	26.6	4.4	6.4	15.8	2.2	19.7	19.9	-0.1
1966	56.6	15.6	25.7	4.3	6.3	15.1	0.7	20.8	19.5	1.3
1967	57.6	16.4	23.1	3.7	5.8	13.6	-0.3	22.2	19.0	3.2
1964-67[1]	56.6	15.5	25.6	4.3	6.2	15.1	1.0	20.6	19.2	1.4
1968	55.9	15.6	23.1	3.8	5.6	13.7	2.1	22.9	19.7	3.3
1969	55.0	15.7	24.2	3.9	5.2	15.1	2.6	23.4	21.0	2.4
1970	53.8	15.9	26.4	4.3	5.4	16.7	2.2	23.1	21.5	1.6
1971	53.9	17.2	26.7	4.1	5.9	16.7	0.8	22.8	21.5	1.3
1968-71[1]	54.7	16.1	25.1	4.0	5.5	15.6	1.9	23.1	20.9	2.2

1. Averages cover periods from first upswing to last downswing years of annual GNP growth during business cycles.

Source : Statistisches Bundesamt.

Chart 1. TRENDS OF GNP AND PRICES

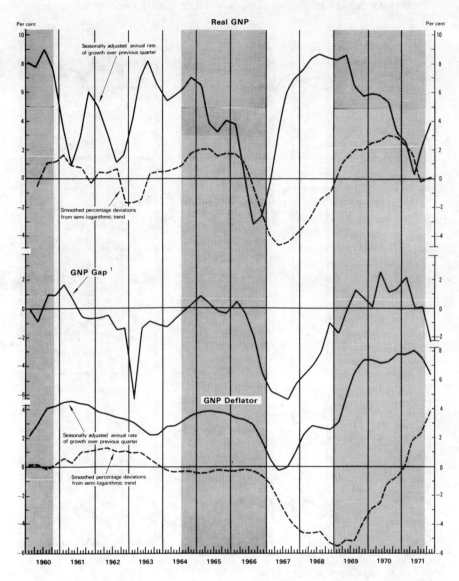

Chart 1. TRENDS OF GNP AND PRICES

1. The GNP gap is defined as the per cent difference between actual output and "potential" output. A negative sign indicates that actual GNP is less than potential and thus that there is some spare capacity. Potential output figures are tentative Secretariat estimates.

NOTE. Shaded parts of all the charts indicate periods of monetary restraint. The method used to identify such periods is explained in Part III, Section (a).

11

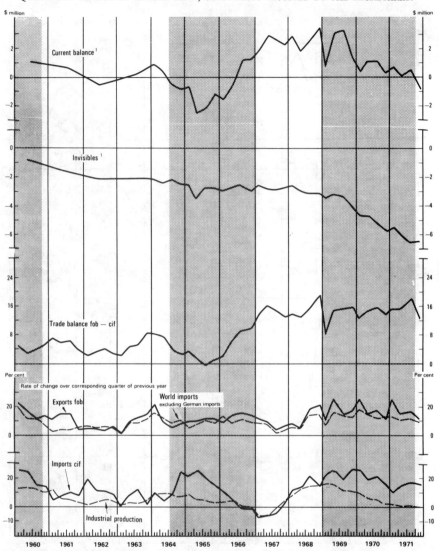

1. Annual figures prior to 1964.

The simple cyclical pattern in the composition of demand should not be viewed solely as the response of the German economy to exogenous shifts in foreign demand. Fluctuations in domestic demand also contributed to a change in the composition of demand in the sense that it was typically possible, perhaps not least due to the latent undervaluation of the mark during most of the period, for German firms to increase foreign sales when the domestic market became less buoyant. On these occasions, the foreign balance acted as an automatic stabiliser diminishing the need for discretionary economic management to encourage economic expansion. On the other hand, the large current surpluses in the economic boom periods of 1960 and 1969-70 had a destabilising effect and underlined the need for revaluations of the deutschemark in 1961, 1969 and 1971. More recently, the current balance of payments position has returned to equilibrium. Long-term capital flows, which were in an outward direction during most of the period under review, assumed increasing proportions, thus offsetting some of the tendencies to surplus on current account (Table 2). However, they have in some instances tended to be disequilibrating. Short-term capital account generally showed net inflows, although the years 1963 and 1967 saw net outflows, and there were violent capital reflows following the revaluation of the mark in the autumn of 1969 and its floating from May through December 1971. These capital flows were to a considerable extent speculative, but differences in monetary conditions between Germany and other financial markets, notably those for short-term assets denominated in Euro-currencies, at times also induced capital movements.

During most of the 1960's, the annual rate of increase of wholesale prices for industrial products in Germany was below that of most other Western European countries and the United States. Similar impressions of somewhat milder inflationary conditions are conveyed by information on consumer prices, GNP price deflator, and unit labour costs (Chart 1). In the light of the very high rate of resource utilisation in Germany, the price performance was clearly better than elsewhere up to 1969. Since then, however, the rate of price increase in Germany has reached or even exceeded the average in other major industrial nations. In a country with memories of two strong inflations within the last half century—1922-23 and the 1940's—this recent experience has brought repeated emphasis on demand management, including monetary policy, with the objective of maintaining international stability.

b) FISCAL POLICY

Prior to 1967 fiscal policy played only a secondary role in demand management. The lack of flexibility in the public sector was due to a number of reasons, among which the very important role of public authorities outside the central government—regional (Länder) governments and local authorities—has remained a lasting element.[1] Indeed the central government constitutes less than half of the public sector; in addition its expenditures are composed in such a way—a high proportion of current purchases and transfers—as to make quick cyclical adjustments difficult. Throughout most of the period up to 1967 the relatively weak role of fiscal policy may not have given rise to concern, because the economy was generally moving smoothly with foreign substituting for domestic demand in periods of slack (see above). But in the cycle of the mid-1960's the impact of the public sector was undoubtedly destabilising. The central government both lowered taxation and increased expenditures in the election year 1965, and regional governments and local authorities increased expend-

---

1. See Bent Hansen, *Fiscal Policy in Seven Countries, 1955-1965,* OECD 1969, pp. 209-12.

TABLE 2. BALAN
U

	1960	1961	1962	1963
Trade balance	2 011	2 405	1 630	2 29:
Invisibles, net	-941	-1 695	-2 118	-2 13(
Current balance.............................	1 070	711	-488	16:
Capital balance	278	147	332	34:
Long-term	-39	-50	-89	38(
Short-term (+ errors and omissions)	317	197	421	-3:
Balance on non-monetary transactions	1 348	858	-156	51(
Balance on official settlements	1 912	792	-220	68(

Source : OECD.

itures as well as borrowing. In 1966-67 the problem was the reverse, as public expenditures were cut back during the weakening of demand and of tax revenues.

In the light of these experiences the Stability and Growth Law[2] was passed by the Bundestag in 1967 when a fiscal stimulus had already been applied along with the easing of monetary policy. The law was intended to ensure that fiscal policy would play a role appropriate to the cyclical situation. It contained various provisions for ensuring that public expenditure, tax policy and borrowing at all levels of government would conform more closely than in the past to anti-cyclical needs. Most of these provisions have, at least to some extent, been used during the recent inflationary period. A notable example has been the building up of counter-cyclical deposits of the Federal and Länder governments with the Bundesbank. They serve the dual purpose of producing counter-cyclical movements in public expenditures and in bank liquidity. In May 1971, limits on borrowing by the main public authorities were imposed for the first time, while the local authorities were requested voluntarily to reduce their borrowing plans.[3]

c) FINANCING BY SECTOR[4]

As already noted on page 13, the overall financial surplus of the German economy (i.e. the balance on current external account) underwent relatively large variations (Chart 3).[5] There was a significant surplus at the beginning of the period; a weakening during the mid-1960's; a swing back

---

2. Gesetz zur Förderung der Stabilität und des Wachstums der Wirtschaft.
3. Under the Stability and Growth Law, regional (Länder) authorities are obliged to take care that local authorities comply with the requirements of the Law. In practice, however, control of fiscal policy behaviour of individual Gemeinden has proved to be difficult.
4. A detailed survey of the German financial structure may be found in *The Capital Market, International Capital Movements, Restrictions on Capital Operations in Germany*, OECD 1969.
5. All data plotted in Charts 3-10 have been deflated by a compound index based on (a) the development of the GNP price deflator and (b) the trend growth of real GNP (calculated by least-squares regression) for the period first half of 1960

1964	1965	1966	1967	1968	1969	1970	1971
2 403	1 300	2 956	5 253	5 676	5 156	5 867	6 369
2 407	−2 981	−2 938	−2 893	−2 950	−3 551	−5 155	−6 201
−3	−1 680	18	2 359	2 725	1 606	730	167
91	1 453	732	−1 071	−1 636	−5 762	2 985	3 520
−259	213	44	−795	−2 901	−5 977	−909	1 754
350	1 240	688	−276	1 265	215	3 894	1 765
88	−227	750	1 288	1 089	−4 156	3`715	3 687
109	−347	606	83	1 703	−2 971	5 881	4 257

into very substantial surplus during the years 1966-69; and in the most recent period a return to approximate balance.

Short-run changes in the external balance were more or less matched by increases or decreases in the net financial deficit of the enterprise sector (see also Chart 6). But three other developments occurred in periods of otherwise close relationship:

    i) in the early 1960's there was a sharp and persistent decline in the net financial surplus of the public authority sector. In 1965 these authorities began collectively to record a net financial deficit;

    ii) over the same period, but only partly offsetting the decline in the public authorities' surplus, households' saving rose substantially faster than GNP. Between 1960 and 1965 the personal savings ratio[6] rose from 8.5 to 12 per cent of personal disposable income. It fell to about 11 per cent during 1966-67 and has since gradually increased to about 13 per cent;

    iii) the financial deficit of the public authority sector increased substantially in 1967, largely reflecting borrowing to finance countercyclical fiscal policies (see pages 13 and 14). But the increase was much less than the decrease in net borrowing by enterprises. In more recent periods, the public authority sector moved back into small net financial surplus, again partly reflecting countercyclical fiscal policies.

Chart 4 illustrates variations in the *flow of borrowing by domestic non-financial sectors* through the domestic credit system. Reflecting the

---

to first half of 1971. In this way cyclical fluctuations are brought out with maximum clarity. Thus, any remaining upward trend for a series indicates that over the period as a whole it was rising faster than GNP; a falling trend means that a series was rising more slowly than GNP, though presumably still increasing in absolute values. Finally, the data were smoothed by a 1-2-1 moving average to take out strong seasonal fluctuations. The method was adapted from one used in a previous analysis of United States flow of funds accounts. See *Flow of Funds Accounts, 1945-1968,* Board of Governors of the Federal Reserve System, pages 1.19-1.21.

    6. Excluding retained profits of non-corporate enterprises.

15

TABLE 3. MATURITY COMPOSITION OF DOMES
DM BILLION (IN BRACKE

	1960	1961	1962	1963
Shorter-term loans[2]	5.4 (66.8)	6.7 (49.8)	5.1 (44.2)	4.4 (42.1
Money market paper[3]	−0.2 (−2.0)	0.3 (2.1)	— (0.1)	0.1 (1.3
Long-term loans	2.9 (35.2)	6.4 (48.1)	6.5 (55.7)	5.8 (56.6
Total	8.1 (100.0)	13.4 (100.0)	11.6 (100.0)	10.3 (100.0

1. Break in series.
2. Bank loans with less than four years' maturity.
3. Issued by Federal Railways and Post Office.
Source: Deutsches Institut für Wirtschaftsforschung.

TABLE 4. SOURCES
PERCENTAGE SHAR

	1960	1961	1962	1963	1964
Mortgage banks	14.5	15.8	18.3	18.0	17.7
Savings banks	16.5	14.7	14.8	15.8	15.8
Building and loan associations	11.5	12.9	12.2	12.9	12.6
Private insurance companies	5.0	5.8	5.1	6.0	6.1
Total financial intermediaries[3]	47.5	49.2	50.4	52.7	52.2
Memorandum item:					
Bond rate[4]	6.6	5.9	6.0	6.1	6.1

1. Break in series.
2. Preliminary.
3. Excluding commercial banks and credit cooperatives.
4. Average yield on new issues of mortgage bonds.
Source: Deutsches Institut fur Wirtschaftsforschung, Deutsche Bundesbank.

features already described, fluctuations of business borrowing were the most important component of total fluctuations. Borrowing to finance housing rose over the period as a whole roughly in line with real GNP. Public authorities' borrowing varied much less than the public authorities' net financial balance, for three reasons. First, in the early 1960's the public authority sector played an important intermediary role, raising funds through the credit system which were loaned on to domestic enterprises; this inter-mediary role still continues, although its relative importance has dimi-nished. Also in the early 1960's the government authorities borrowed substantially from the domestic credit system to pay off foreign indebted-

1964	1965	1966	1967	1968	1969[1]	1970	1971
5.9	7.7	7.7	1.5	4.9	20.0	15.9	20.8
(50.8)	(57.1)	(71.0)	(19.5)	(31.6)	(56.2)	(54.0)	(55.7)
—	—	—	-0.2	-0.3	0.5	-0.2	-0.5
(-0.3)	(0.3)	(-0.1)	(-2.7)	(-1.9)	(1.3)	(-0.5)	(-1.3)
5.7	5.7	3.2	6.5	11.0	15.2	13.7	17.1
(49.5)	(42.6)	(29.1)	(83.2)	(70.3)	(42.5)	(46.5)	(45.6)
11.6	13.4	10.9	7.8	15.6	35.7	29.4	37.4
(100.0)	(100.0)	(100.0)	(100.0)	(100.0)	(100.0)	(100.0)	(100.0)

1965	1966	1967	1967[1]	1968	1969	1970	1971[a]
15.9	12.5	14.8	13.0	15.2	15.1	11.8	12.6
16.3	15.6	16.6	14.5	16.2	17.2	13.6	12.8
15.2	17.4	15.5	11.8	11.1	17.0	18.6	15.5
7.0	8.6	9.0	6.6	6.4	6.6	6.5	7.1
54.4	54.1	55.9	45.9	47.9	56.1	50.5	48.0
7.0	7.9	7.0	7.0	6.7	6.8	8.1	8.0

ness, or to finance government lending abroad. Finally, a substantial part of the deterioration in the public authorities' financial position during the mid-1960's was financed by a running down of accumulated financial assets.

Borrowing by the *business sector* is illustrated in Chart 7. Clearly apparent is the predominance of variations in bank loans in the total variation of funds obtained through the domestic credit system. Total borrowing by the business sector varied even more than borrowing in domestic financial markets. This reflected variations in the flow of funds lent by public authorities and by the rest of the world. The data include direct foreign investment in German companies, but—particularly in recent

17

periods—the main fluctuations were (recorded or unrecorded) short-term borrowing abroad. Another noticeable phenomenon has been fluctuations in the maturity composition of borrowing by the business sector (Table 3). Short-term liabilities have tended to gain in weight during periods of credit restraint and have been consolidated to some extent in periods of monetary ease.

The banking system (especially the savings and mortgage banks) is furthermore the main source of funds borrowed to finance *housing* (Chart 8). The supply of funds for housing by banks has tended to move counter-cyclically (Table 4). But the declines have at times, notably in the mid-1960's, been partly offset by increases in the volume of finance provided by building and loan associations (see pages 19 and 71). Interest rate subsidies and other financial assistance by the public authorities have also tended to dampen the impact on housing finance from monetary restraint.[7]

A breakdown of borrowing by the *public authorities* is shown in Chart 9. Bank loans were the more important form of borrowing throughout most of the period, developing roughly in line with GNP. The public sector debt was substantially reduced by the post-war monetary reform; although the financial needs of the public sector have been gradually increasing since then, they have not been large in relation to national output: at the end of 1971 internal government debt (excluding that of local authorities) was equivalent to about 15 per cent of GNP in that year. The structure of public sector debt is shown in Table 5. Only a relatively small part consists of government bills or bonds: hence the problem of maintaining stability in the prices of marketable debt has not constrained monetary policy as it has, at times, in certain other countries. The structure of public debt shifted in 1967-68 when expansionary fiscal policies were financed by short-term securities; but there was a shift back towards longer-term debt in 1969-70.[8]

The *household sector* is predominant among the sectors with a financial surplus (Chart 3); relative to GNP its lending to other sectors has increased steadily and strongly during the period. The pattern of its financial holdings has not changed much (Table 6). Time and savings deposits placed with banks have accounted for about half of the total increase in financial assets, direct purchases of securities for less than one-fifth, only slightly more than contractual savings through insurance. There has been no clear trend in purchases of securities; but households' portfolio behaviour seems to have undergone a marked change during the past decade. While the household sector tended to reduce bond purchases when bond yields approached their cyclical peak and for some time maintained a "wait-and-see" attitude in subsequent periods of rising bond prices,[9] the sharp rise in bond yields in 1970 was accompanied by a considerable increase in purchases of fixed-interest securities by private households. Purchases then remained high in the following year. The earlier "perverse" reaction and

---

7. The direct, but limited, role of the local public authorities in housing construction will not be reviewed in the present study.

8. On the more technical aspects of this period of active debt management, see Appendix I.

9. The 1961 data are in part masked by purchases of shares in connection with the denationalisation of Volkswagenwerke.

18

high liquidity preference may thus have been replaced by a more sophisticated response of household purchases to changes in relative interest rates comparable to that observed in some other industrial countries. Household saving has been encouraged by a number of incentive schemes including both deductibility from taxable income for amounts saved up to a ceiling and transfers to savers in the form of premiums. There is some evidence to suggest that these measures have contributed to the increase in household saving since 1962.

d) FINANCIAL INSTITUTIONS AND MARKETS

The role of *banks* is dominant in the German financial system. The main type of bank is the "all purpose" bank (Universalbank) which engages in all types of banking business (Table 7); it accepts deposits in the full range of maturities and raises additional funds through the issue of bank debentures, and it grants short, medium and long-term loans. Banks are an important—and at times even dominant—group of buyers in the bond market and act as dealers and as issuing houses in the securities market; they hold interests especially in joint stock companies, are members of supervisory boards and play an important role in representing non-bank shareholders' interests in companies' annual meetings. Financial and institutional links between the banking system and the business sector thus are manifold. There is at the present time no clear distinction between commercial and savings banks, though the latter continue to rely more on long-term deposits and to lend more on a longer-term basis, satisfying primarily credit needs of local authorities, smaller enterprises and residential construction. In recent years the savings banks, and particularly their central institutions (the "Girozentralen") have moved into lending to large enterprises and participation in issuing syndicates, the traditional preserve of the commercial banks. The private and public mortgage banks rely heavily on issues of debentures which they mainly use to finance long-term loans, publicly guaranteed credits and loans to the public sector. The remaining institutions grouped in the banking sector are mainly various categories of credit co-operatives and their central institutions.

The relative importance of the banking system and of bank loans increased after 1967 (Chart 5). The collapse of bond prices in 1966-67 temporarily reinforced the preference for financial assets (mainly time deposits) not subject to fluctuations in value, and the removal in early 1967 of limits on the rates of interest payable on bank deposits also helped the collection of bank deposits. Another factor tending, in recent years, to increase the importance of banks has been the growing amount of long-term note issues (Schuldscheindarlehen) by private and public borrowers in place of long-term bond issues. These instruments, which are purchased mainly by banks and insurance companies, and not sold to the general public, provide a cheaper and more flexible source of financing than the issue of bonds.

The group of *non-bank financial intermediaries* comprises building and loan associations, insurance companies and social security funds. Building and loan associations receive long-term deposits and grant building loans to their depositors; the growth of their activity has been relatively

TABLE 5. STRUCTURE OF PUBL

		Borrowing from Bundesbank		Treasury bills[2]
		Book credits	Special credits[1]	
A. *Outstanding at end-year* DM billion (in brackets per cent of total)				
1. Federal and Länder authorities	1959	0.2 (0.6)	0.1 (0.1)	0.5 (1.2)
	1965	1.4 (2.5)	2.3 (4.1)	1.3 (2.1)
	1968	1.3 (1.6)	0.8 (1.0)	8.7 (10.6)
	1971	2.3 (2.5)	.. (0)	1.7 (1.8)
of which: Federal authorities	1959	0.2 (1.0)	0.1 (0.2)	0.3 (1.2)
	1965	1.1 (2.7)	2.3 (5.9)	1.2 (3.0)
	1968	1.3 (2.4)	0.8 (1.4)	8.5 (15.0)
	1971	1.7 (2.9)	—	—
2. Local authorities	1959	—	—	—
	1965	—	—	—
	1968	—	—	—
	1971	—	—	—
B. *Changes* DM billion				
1. Federal and Länder authorities	1959-65	1.2	2.3	0.9
	1965-68	−0.1	−1.5	7.4
	1968-71	1.0	−0.7	−7.1
of which: Federal authorities	1959-65	0.8	2.3	0.9
	1965-68	0.3	−1.5	7.3
	1968-71	0.4	−0.8	−8.5
2. Local authorities	1959-65	—	—	—
	1965-68	—	—	—
	1968-71	—	—	—

1. Credits to the Federal authorities to finance the repayment of external debt and for subscriptions to international organisations (excluding the IMF) and claims in respect of changes in the exchange parity.
2. Including Treasury bonds of up to two years' maturity sold at a discount from par.

Source : Deutsche Bundesbank.

Medium term notes	Long-term bonds	Bank loans	Loans from domestic non-banks[3]	Other domestic debt[4]	Foreign	Total
0.7 (1.8)	2.8 (7.0)	2.4 (6.1)	2.5 (6.4)	23.5 (59.5)	6.9 (17.4)	39.5 (100.0)
1.2 (2.0)	10.6 (18.6)	4.8 (8.4)	7.7 (13.5)	24.6 (43.0)	3.3 (5.7)	57.2 (100.0)
4.0 (4.9)	15.3 (18.4)	17.0 (20.5)	9.6 (11.6)	24.2 (29.2)	1.9 (2.3)	82.9 (100.0)
2.6 (2.8)	19.4 (21.0)	31.5 (34.1)	11.3 (12.2)	22.4 (24.3)	1.3 (1.4)	92.4 (100.0)
0.6) (2.4)	1.0 (4.3)	0.5 (2.0)	1.1 (4.4)	14.0 (57.0)	6.7 (27.3)	24.5 (100.0)
1.2 (2.9)	8.0 (20.0)	1.3 (3.2)	5.8 (14.6)	15.8 (39.8)	3.1 (7.8)	39.8 (100.0)
3.5 (6.1)	9.8 (17.3)	8.2 (14.5)	6.8 (12.0)	16.0 (28.2)	1.8 (3.2)	56.6 (100.0)
2.3 (3.8)	12.5 (21.0)	17.6 (29.7)	7.6 (12.8)	14.8 (25.0)	1.2 2.0	59.4 (100.0)
—	0.3 (3.2)	7.0 (73.1)	2.2 (22.8)	—	0.1 (0.9)	9.6 (100.0)
—	0.6 (2.2)	20.0 (77.2)	5.2 (20.3)	—	0.1 (0.2)	25.8 (100.0)
—	0.8 (2.3)	26.8 (78.4)	6.6 (19.2)	—	.. (0.1)	34.2 (100.0)
—	0.9 (1.8)	39.0 (81.1)	8.2 (17.1)	—	.. (0)	48.1 (100.0)
0.5	7.8	2.4	5.2	1.0	–3.6	17.7
2.9	4.7	12.2	1.9	–0.4	–1.3	25.8
–1.5	4.1	14.5	1.6	–0.8	–0.7	9.5
0.5	6.9	0.8	4.7	1.9	–3.6	15.2
2.3	1.8	6.9	1.0	0.1	–1.3	16.8
–1.2	2.7	9.4	0.8	–1.1	–0.6	2.8
—	0.3	12.9	3.1	—	..	16.2
—	0.2	6.8	1.3	—	..	8.3
—	0.1	12.2	1.7	—	..	13.9

3. Direct loans from social security institutions and other lenders.
4. Debts originating in the Currency Reform (through consolidation of claims on the former regime) or through arrangements for repayment of the same.

TABLE 6. CHANGES IN FINANCI

	1960	1961	1962	1963
1. *Bank deposits and currency*	*9.4*	*9.6*	*10.3*	*13.2*
1.1. Sight deposits and currency	1.9	2.7	1.6	1.7
1.2. Time and savings deposits	7.5	6.9	8.8	11.5
2. *Funds placed with non-bank financial intermediaries*	*4.6*	*5.2*	*5.5*	*6.0*
2.1. With insurance companies	2.9	3.3	3.8	4.0
2.2. With building and loan associations	1.8	1.9	1.7	2.0
3. *Purchases of securities*	*2.3*	*3.7*	*3.4*	*3.6*
3.1. Bonds	1.0	1.4	2.7	3.5
3.2. Shares	1.3	2.3	0.7	0.1
4. *Total financial assets*	*16.5*	*18.6*	19.3	22.9
1. *Bank deposits and currency*	*57*	*52*	*54*	*58*
1.1. Sight deposits and currency	12	15	8	8
1.2. Time and savings deposits	46	37	46	50
2. *Funds placed with non-bank financial intermediaries*	*28*	*28*	*28*	*26*
2.1. With insurance companies	17	18	20	18
2.2. With building and loan associations	11	10	9	9
3. *Purchases of securities*	*14*	*20*	*18*	*16*
3.1. Bonds	6	7	14	15
3.2. Shares	8	12	4	..
4. *Total financial assets*	*100*	*100*	*100*	*100*

NOTE. Detail may not add due to rounding.
.. Less than 0.5 per cent.
Source : Deutsche Bundesbank.

rapid due to the strong demand for housing and various government support measures to building activity. The insurance sector, too, lends primarily to construction, though loans to industry are also significant.

Funds flowing through the *bond market* directly to non-financial borrowers were a relatively small and stable component of total borrowing (Chart 10) and, as such, made but a minor contribution to the financing of industry. But the bond market played an important role as a channel for flows of funds within the banking system and, particularly in 1963, 1967-69 and 1971-72, as a vehicle for the international flow of long-term capital. Households have, on average, been the main net purchasers

1964	1965	1966	1967	1968	1969	1970	1971
DM BILLION							
15.6	19.4	18.8	19.0	24.5	26.2	26.8	35.7
2.7	2.7	2.0	1.3	2.4	3.7	4.2	5.9
12.9	16.7	16.8	17.6	22.1	22.5	22.6	29.8
6.6	8.2	9.8	8.7	9.1	11.1	12.7	15.2
4.4	4.9	5.5	6.1	6.7	7.3	7.6	10.0
2.1	3.3	4.3	2.6	2.4	3.8	5.1	5.2
6.0	7.0	3.3	4.0	4.7	8.8	11.1	8.7
5.4	4.7	2.4	2.8	3.1	5.5	9.5	7.1
0.6	2.2	0.9	1.3	1.5	3.3	1.6	1.6
28.3	34.7	32.0	31.8	38.4	46.1	50.7	59.6
PER CENT							
55	56	59	60	64	57	53	60
10	8	6	4	6	8	8	10
45	48	53	56	58	49	45	50
23	24	31	27	24	24	25	26
16	14	17	19	18	16	15	17
8	10	13	8	6	8	10	9
21	20	10	13	12	19	22	15
19	14	8	9	8	12	19	12
2	7	3	4	4	7	3	3
100	100	100	100	100	100	100	100

of bonds, but their participation in the market fluctuated cyclically and was, at times, outweighed by bank participation. In the early years of the decade, social security institutions were also fairly important purchasers of bonds, but, since 1966, their purchases have been negligible or negative, reflecting the changes in regulations concerning bond purchases by these institutions. Foreigners were also significant purchasers of bonds in the early years of the 1960's and in 1971-72. But since the announcement of the Withholding Tax in 1964 foreigners have, in most years, been net sellers. During most of the period, variations in bank portfolio invest- ments were of crucial importance in determining short-run fluctuations in

23

TABLE 7. BANKING SYSTEM: PRINCIPA

	Volume of business DM billion	Inter-bank[1]	Main categories	
			Ot	
			Sight deposits	Time deposits
All banks	*924.5*	*24*	*9*	*15*
Commercial banks	232.8	33	15	23
Savings banks	211.5	9	13	6
Central giro institutions	141.6	36	2	13
Mortgage banks	123.0	11	..	27
All other	215.6	30	8	13
All banks	*100*	*100*	*100*	*100*
Commercial banks	25	34	41	37
Savings banks	23	8	33	9
Central giro institutions	15	23	4	12
Mortgage banks	13	6	..	23
All other	23	29	22	19

1. Including liabilities to the Bundesbank and to foreign banks, but excluding bonds held by banks, for which a sectoral breakdown by issuers is not available.
2. Including bonds held by other banks; see note 1.
3. Including claims on foreign banks.
4. Treasury bills (excluding mobilisation paper), other discounted bills and loans and advances for less than 12 months.

bond yields and the demand for fixed-interest securities, since private households tended, until recently, to reduce their purchases in response to a decline in bank participation and the concomitant fall in bond prices. The German *share market* is of about the same size, as a source of funds for non-financial borrowers, as the bond market. Share issues have tended to rise when bond issues have fallen and vice versa; examples may be found in 1965 and 1969. Foreigners have been active on both sides of the market, supplying funds net during most of the 1960's and in 1970-71; net sales in 1968 and the subsequent years were followed by some buying in 1970 and very large buying in 1971 and in the first half of 1972.

In summary, the main characteristics of the German financial system are the crucial role of the banking system and the stability in the pattern of flows through domestic financial markets, notwithstanding large fluctuations in the total amounts borrowed or changes in monetary policy. This is the case both for total borrowing and for the two largely private sectors

ilities		Main categories of assets					
					Other		
Savings deposits	Bonds²	Inter-bank³	of which: bank bonds	Short-term loans⁴	Medium and long-term loans	Securities⁶
N PER CENT OF VOLUME OF BUSINESS							
26	15	26	6	16	47	3
18	4	25	3	31	26	5
66	—	25	14	13	50	1
1	39	31	5	9	53	3
..	47	7	1	1	89	1
26	5	35	7	14	40	2
PER CENT OF BANKING SYSTEM TOTALS							
100	100	100	100	100	100	100
17	7	25	13	51	14	50
58	—	22	48	18	24	12
1	41	18	13	9	17	15
—	43	4	1	1	25	4
24	9	32	25	22	20	20

5. Excluding bank bonds.
— Nil.
.. Less than 0.5 per cent.
Source : Deutsche Bundesbank.

—enterprises and housebuilding. This apparent stability may, in part, reflect specific attitudes of German wealth holders (see page 18); but part of it would seem to reflect choices by borrowers as to the types of liabilities they are prepared to incur. One factor is the close link between many German companies and particular banks; and between Länder and local authorities and savings banks and their central giro institutions. Such links may, to a certain extent, inhibit these borrowers from exploring untraditional channels or forms of financing. Also important, until recently, was a deliberate policy choice to restrict sales of short-term government paper mainly to the banking system, one reason for this being the Bundesbank's wish to avoid competition with the banks for deposits. The very brief survey above has also identified such structural elements as the short-run variations in the supply of long-term bank loans and the changing absorption capacity of the bond market accompanying monetary policy changes.

25

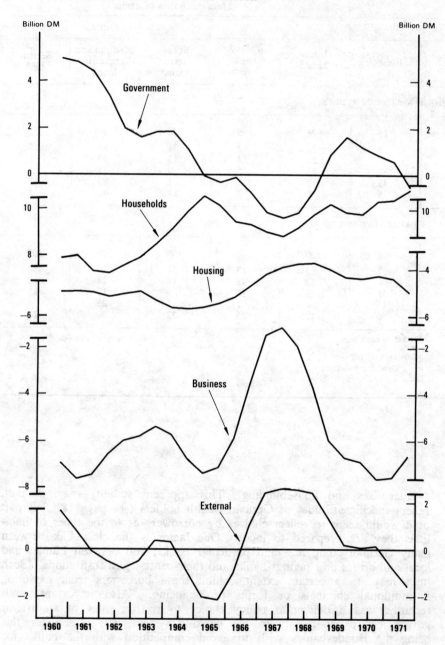

Chart 3. FINANCIAL SURPLUSES AND DEFICITS
By sector

Billion DM

Billion DM

Government

Households

Housing

Business

External

1960 1961 1962 1963 1964 1965 1966 1967 1968 1969 1970 1971

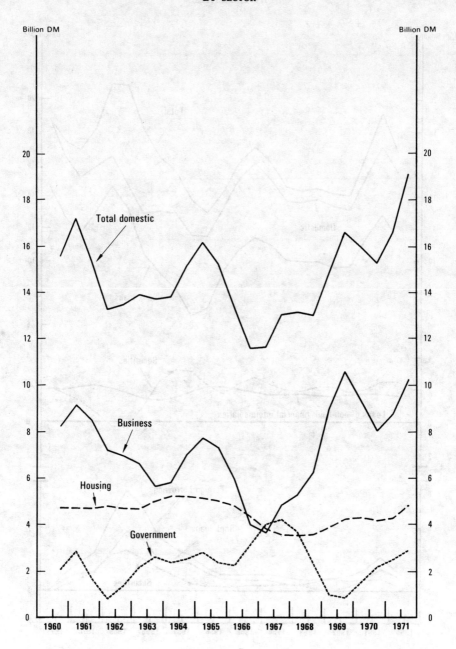

Chart 4. CREDIT FLOWS TO DOMESTIC NON-FINANCIAL SECTORS
BY SECTOR

Billion DM

Billion DM

Total domestic

Business

Housing

Government

1960   1961   1962   1963   1964   1965   1966   1967   1968   1969   1970   1971

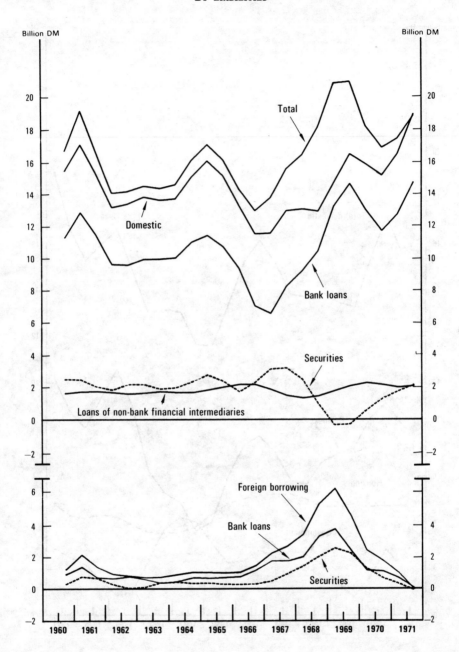

Chart 6. BUSINESS SECTOR'S GROSS AND NET SAVINGS
AND INVESTMENT

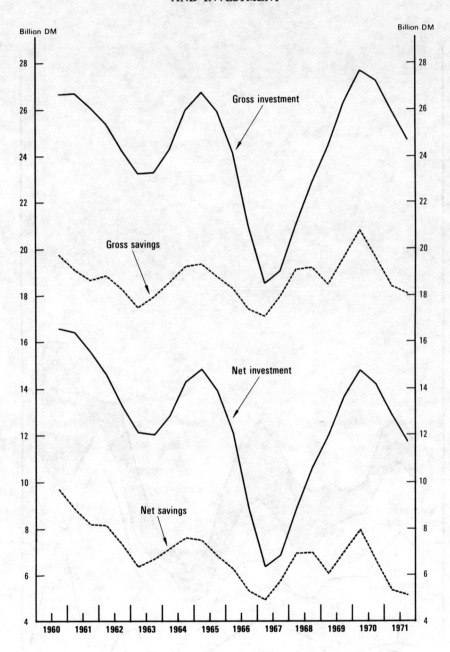

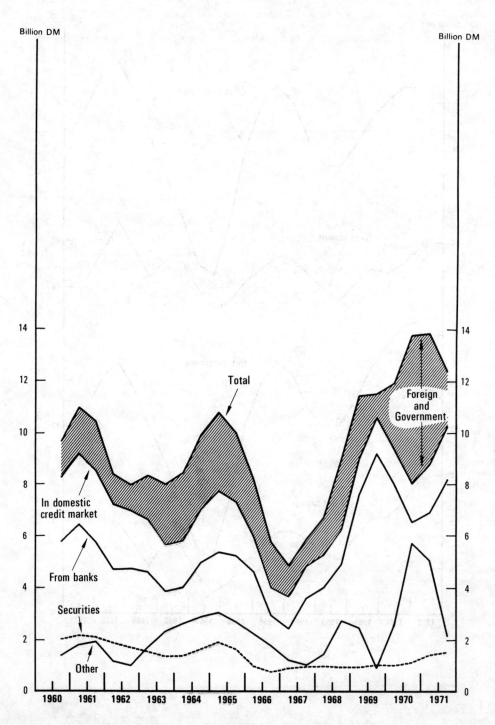

Chart 7. BUSINESS SECTOR'S BORROWING
By types

Billion DM

Billion DM

Total

Foreign
and
Government

In domestic
credit market

From banks

Securities

Other

14

12

10

8

6

4

2

0

14

12

10

8

6

4

2

0

1960 1961 1962 1963 1964 1965 1966 1967 1968 1969 1970 1971

30

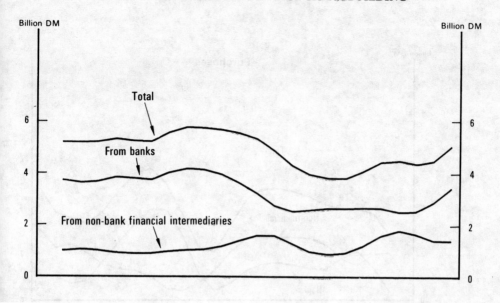

Chart 8. BORROWING TO FINANCE HOUSEBUILDING

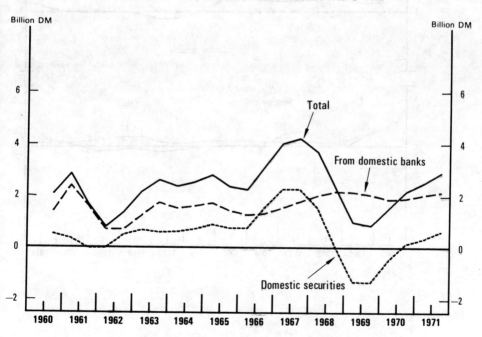

Chart 9. PUBLIC SECTOR'S BORROWING

31

Chart 10. T

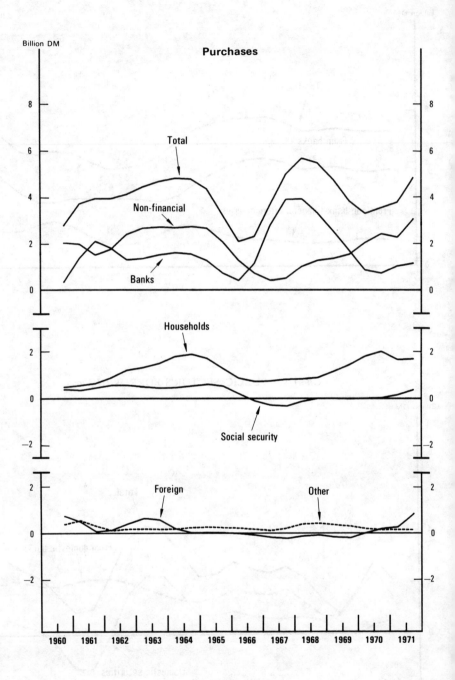

Billion DM

Purchases

8

6   Total

4   Non-financial

2

Banks

0

Households

2

0

Social security

−2

Foreign   Other

2

0

−2

1960 1961 1962 1963 1964 1965 1966 1967 1968 1969 1970 1971

32

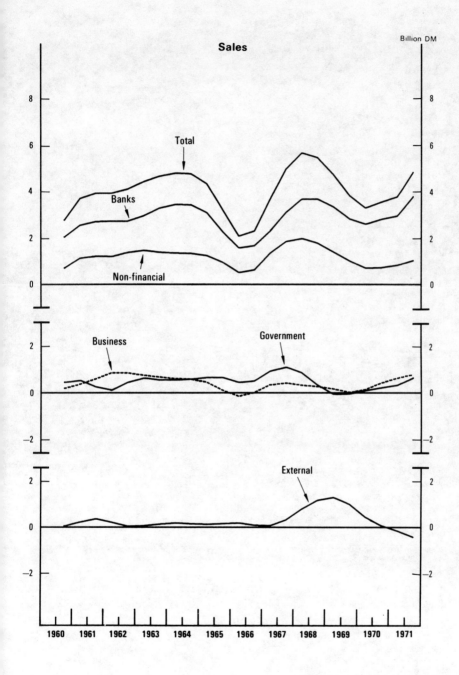

Sales

Billion DM

II

INSTRUMENTS OF MONETARY POLICY
AND OPERATING TARGETS

a) INSTRUMENTS OF MONETARY POLICY

The Bundesbank possesses a number of monetary instruments. The following paragraphs review the main features of these instruments and their use, while leaving a more detailed description to the Appendices.[1]

Discount rate policy has traditionally been a most important monetary instrument. The rate has been changed more than 20 times since the beginning of 1960. It applies to all bills which are eligible under the Bundesbank Act; an earlier preferential rate for foreign and export bills was discontinued in 1956. Changes in the discount rate and in the rate charged for advances on securities and certain claims against the public sector—the latter (the Lombard rate) has usually been varied in step with the discount rate at a level $\frac{1}{2}$ to 3 percentage points above it[2]—have typically been aimed at influencing money market rates and, notably before 1967, bank lending and deposit rates. Day-to-day and call money rates on the interbank market in which the Bundesbank does not participate, are, in particular, conditioned by the prevailing Lombard rate. In periods of tight monetary policy when many banks have (or are close to having) used up their rediscount quotas and are indebted to the central bank under Lombard arrangements, the Lombard rate acts as a floor to the interbank rate, since banks will want to repay Bundesbank borrowing when the two rates are not far apart. Conversely in periods of easy monetary policy, the Lombard rate has operated as a ceiling, since banks have no incentive to borrow in the money market if rates rise above the cost of easily accessible central bank advances. A similar mechanism tends to link one and three months money market rates with the official discount rate. In both situations, therefore, changes in policy are likely to be immediately felt in the money market, thus reinforcing the impact of discount and Lombard rate changes on interest rates charged to ultimate borrowers.

Before April 1967 the maximum and actual rates that banks charged their customers tended to be automatically raised with changes in the

---

1. See also *Instruments of Monetary Policy in the Federal Republic of Germany,* Deutsche Bundesbank, 1971.
2. In recent years fluctuations in the Lombard rate have tended to become sharper, as banks had more heavy recourse to Lombard credit; in late 1969 it was increased, at one stage, to 3 percentage points above the discount rate.

discount rate; for example, the maximum rate[3] chargeable on current account credits—the main form of bank lending to the business sector—was fixed at 4½ percentage points above the discount rate. Since interest rates were liberalised and, in principle, became determined by competition, the differential has typically remained in the range of 4-5 percentage points above the discount rate, lower immediately after increases in discount rate changes, higher after reductions. The impact of such changes therefore seems to have been modified with respect to timing rather than to strength. The aim of the 1967 reform was to remove some of the rigidity of the interest rate structure while retaining ample scope for influencing rates through more indirect market adjustments to changes in the cost of Bundesbank credit. These transmission mechanisms will be reviewed in Part III on the impact of monetary policy on financial variables.

Changes in rediscount quotas have been another important policy instrument. Within these quotas, the access of banks to central bank credit is virtually automatic at the prevailing discount rate. Each bank has a standard quota which has generally been related to the size of its capital, though somewhat different formulas have been applicable to different types of banks. The absolute figure for the quotas, therefore, has shown a tendency to grow over time, though a series of global reductions at intervals during the period exerted a moderating influence. From the banks' point of view, a cut in quotas has the advantage of not directly diminishing profits, as might well be the consequence of a requirement to increase non-interest bearing deposits with the Bundesbank; but the relatively long warning with which quotas have typically been reduced testifies to the importance attached to this narrowing of a major route of access to the lender of last resort. From time to time, qualitative rules defining which bills are eligible for rediscounting have also been changed. While such changes typically have some effect in restraining credit to particular classes of bank borrowers, e.g. builders or consumers, there is less reason to believe that they have significantly restrained total credit, since the banks have never been short of eligible paper within their quotas; but there may have been indirect effects throughout.

Advances on securities and certain claims against the public sector (Lombard credits), another way in which private banks borrow from the Bundesbank, are meant to be only short-run finance and must be repaid within 30 days. Although the Bundesbank has clear rules listing eligible assets and the percentage of their nominal value which can be used as collateral, the granting of advances depends on the general credit situation as well as on the position of the individual borrowers. Lack of automatic recourse to the Bundesbank and the requirement of early repayment were rather strictly observed policy principles until the end of the 1960's. In August 1970, the rule was established that the monthly average of advances against collateral should generally not exceed 20 per cent of banks' rediscount quotas, and in May 1973 Lombard credits were suspended altogether until further notice.

Changes in minimum reserve requirements have been the instrument most frequently used in Germany. During the period under study these

---

3. Data are not available on rates actually charged before the statutory ceilings were abolished.

requirements have been changed more than 30 times. In principle, all banks must maintain certain minimum reserves, but the Bundesbank Act makes it possible to differentiate by category of institution and deposit liability. The structure of the reserve requirement has accordingly become very complex with a very wide array of percentages. Usually, however, requirements against domestic liabilities are changed by a uniform percentage; but generally higher and more variable requirements have been applied to non-resident liabilities. The minimum reserve requirement (Mindest-Reserve-Soll) is determined by applying the ratios fixed by the Bundesbank to the average of a bank's liabilities over a four weeks' assessment period between calendar months; the banks have the option of calculating this average on the basis of only four daily positions spread evenly over the period.[4] The regulations leave banks some flexibility in managing their reserves, since compliance with the requirements is measured on the basis of monthly averages of daily reserve holdings and excludes the need for additional working balances (excess reserves) with the Bundesbank. No interest is paid on required reserves; a penal rate of 3 per cent above the rate on advances is charged on any shortfall in meeting the requirement.

While changes in average reserve requirements against domestic deposits, notably sight liabilities, have retained their importance throughout the period, increasing use has been made in the period since late 1968 of changes in average and marginal requirements against liabilities to non-residents. In 1968-69 the latter ratio was put at its maximum of 100 per cent, while the average ratio remained at levels comparable to those against domestic liabilities. At other times of substantial capital inflows —1961, 1964 and 1971—also the average ratio against non-residents liabilities has been increased sharply.[5]

In addition to these instruments, *open market operations* have also been used in Germany, but less frequently. Operations were until recently conducted almost entirely in money market paper between the banks and the Bundesbank with the latter fixing the terms on which it was prepared to sell (or buy) and with the buyer (or seller) determining the volume of transactions.[6] Up to mid-1971, although generally small amounts of money market paper were at times sold to and bought from a selected group of non-bank institutions (public social security institutions and the Post Office), the Bundesbank deliberately refrained from creating a general market in money market instruments outside the banks (see Appendix I), and in fixing short-term interest rates it never offered rates above prevailing deposit rates. Since 1967 the Bundesbank has used its authority to deal in long-term securities. The latter type of operations reached sizeable proportions in 1967-68 when the Bundesbank purchased public authority bonds which were in ample supply because of the generally reflationary policies pursued during this phase; but in early 1969 the Bundesbank reverted to its earlier policy of not interfering directly in the long-term market by announcing that it would no longer make purchases on its

---

4. This option was abandoned in respect of foreign demand deposit liabilities in May 1972.

5. For the extension of reserve requirements to slow down the inflow of non-banking funds, see the discussion of the Bardepot in pages 38 and 66.

6. There is no need at this point to go into the arrangements by which the Bundesbank is enabled at any time to have an adequate portfolio of money market instruments; see Appendix I.

own account. It was felt that the other available instruments offered sufficient scope for monetary management and that the heavy involvement of the banks in the bond market assured a quick transmission of changes in money market conditions to the bond market and to long-term interest rates (this view will be examined on page 67 below). More recently the Bundesbank has begun gradually to abandon its earlier policy principles about operations in money market paper: since mid-1971 such paper is offered for sale to the general public. This new approach to open market policy was underlined in the second half of 1972 when the Bundesbank's selling rates were made effectively competitive in relation to banks' deposit rates.

Since 1958 the Bundesbank has at times offered German banks the possibility of *swap transactions in US dollars* for periods between 15 and 180 days. The Bundesbank has been selling dollars spot to the banks and buying them back forward at rates usually more favourable than those available in the market to other forward market participants; in the 1967-69 period when interest rates in the United States and the Euro-dollar market were higher than in Germany (Chart 18), this implied a smaller discount on the dollar than the sizeable one prevailing in the market; but at other times the forward dollar has been quoted at par or at a small premium. In brief periods in 1968 and 1970-71 the Bundesbank also intervened in the regular forward market. The purpose of making short-term dollar investments relatively more attractive was, originally, to encourage the participation of the German banks in international financial markets; in most instances where swap facilities have been widely used, the motive of the German authorities has been to dampen the increase in official international reserves while maintaining domestic short-term rates at levels desirable from the domestic viewpoint. In 1967, maintenance of an expansionary policy stance was hampered by tight monetary conditions abroad inducing unwanted short-term outflows. In these conditions the Bundesbank forced up the dollar spot rate, widening at the same time the margin between its buying and selling rates in order to encourage the development of a high discount on the forward dollar.

Apart from exchange market intervention, the authorities resorted to a number of *specific external policy expedients* to prevent or discourage undesirable short-term capital inflows which tended to undermine domestic policies of credit restraint. Such techniques were partly devised within its authority by the Bundesbank, while others were introduced and implemented in close cooperation between the government and the central bank. Until recently, the main emphasis was on the control of short-term capital flows through the domestic banking system. To this end, existing policy instruments were adjusted, involving in particular specific modifications in minimum reserve requirement ratios (see pages 36 and 37), exemptions from reserve requirements on bank liabilities to non-residents invested in short-term foreign assets, and reductions of rediscount quotas corresponding to increases in certain external liabilities other than foreign deposits. In addition interest payments on non-resident deposits, acquisition by non-residents of domestic money market paper and of domestic bonds under repurchase agreements, bank borrowing abroad and acceptance of deposits from non-residents were temporarily made subject to licensing (Table 10), and banks were requested to notify the central bank

38

of sales of domestic credit claims to non-residents. Inflows of foreign portfolio capital were dampened by the introduction of a withholding tax on income from non-resident holdings of German bonds and, in 1972, by subjecting the sale of domestic bonds to non-residents to licensing. In February 1973 these controls were extended to include non-residents' purchase of all domestic securities from residents. Furthermore, the guaranteeing by domestic banks of companies' foreign liabilities was temporarily restricted, and the 1972 Cash Deposits Law has subjected such liabilities to cash deposits at the central bank in order to raise the effective cost to enterprises of borrowing abroad.

As will become evident from the following review of how monetary policy was actually used, this survey of monetary instruments excludes one variable, exchange rate policy, which has been more important than any other in determining the climate in which German monetary policy has had to operate. The deutschemark was revalued three times during the period under study (in 1961, 1969 and 1971 by 5, 9.3 and 13.6 per cent respectively vis-à-vis the dollar), and twice in 1973 (by 3 and $5\frac{1}{2}$ per cent in terms of its central rate vis-à-vis the other European currencies which are jointly floating against the dollar). The widespread belief in Germany and abroad, during a shorter or longer period prior to each of these exchange rate adjustments, that the mark was undervalued generated very large speculative inflows of capital which greatly complicated the task of the German monetary authorities; and revaluation was partly followed by dramatic reflows of capital. Some of these interactions between capital flows and monetary conditions in Germany are reviewed in Part III.

b) MAIN OPERATING TARGETS

Throughout most of the period since 1960, with the instruments available to them, the German monetary authorities have sought to attain their policy objectives, on the one hand, by acting on interest rates on bank lending and deposits and on the money and capital markets and, on the other, by action on "bank liquidity" ("free liquid reserves" of the banking system).

Until recently, the definition of the volume of bank liquidity[7] comprised the following five components:

 i) excess balances with the Bundesbank;
 ii) domestic money market paper;
 iii) money market investment abroad;[8]
 iv) unused rediscount margins[9] and, as a negative item,
 v) short-term Bundesbank advances against collateral.

The latter component was deducted because of lack of automatic recourse to this type of central bank credit and the requirement of early repayment

---

7. A detailed description of the sources and uses of bank liquidity may be found in Appendix I.

8. Since February 1973, this component has been excluded from the definition of bank liquidity.

9. Before February 1973, rediscounting was automatic within unused rediscount quotas; use of rediscount facilities has thereafter been limited to 60 per cent of the existing quotas.

(see page 36).[10] This measure does not correspond to either of the concepts of total, unborrowed or net free reserves in use in some other countries, notably the United States. The German concept excludes required reserves, which form the major part of total (or of unborrowed) primary reserves, but does not deduct short-term foreign liabilities; thus it is a net measure of liquidity only to the extent that it nets out the short-term advances granted by the Bundesbank. Only a small proportion consists of primary money, but the remainder may be converted into such at the Bundesbank. It is this inclusion of some parts of secondary liquidity which gives the German measure its special flavour; it is an indication of the banks' scope for widening the monetary base by mobilising additional liquidity and, thus, the potential lending capacity of the banking system, rather than a measure of their current reserve position.

The use of this specific measure of bank liquidity in preference to various concepts of banks' prime reserve positions was closely linked to bank behaviour and institutional arrangements in Germany which have partly reflected deliberate policy choices by the monetary authorities:

i) Given quasi-automatic access to the supply of base money, secondary liquid reserves carry a degree of "moneyness" similar to that of excess primary reserves; this enabled both groups of liquid assets to be subsumed in a single measure of bank liquidity.

ii) In the short run, by definition a period not exceeding a calendar month, balances held with the Bundesbank were allowed to vary from the monthly average level of required reserves (see page 36); until recently, the Bundesbank refrained from smoothing out short-run fluctuations in banks' primary reserves. Thus the banking system's current reserve position is largely endogenously determined and cannot be a short-run target for monetary policy.

iii) Over the month, banks' average balances held with the Bundesbank rarely exceeded required reserves to any significant extent. This was partly due to the banks' reluctance to maintain excess reserves, for which the possibility of quasi-automatic access to the supply of base money has probably been a close substitute. It also reflected the limited use by the Bundesbank of active open market operations to produce desired changes in the banks' primary reserve position. Under these circumstances, any concept of bank reserves would not seem to be a useful operating target.

How useful the measure is in monetary management can only be determined in the light of observed behavioural relationships for the German banks (see Part III below). The aim is obviously to define as reliably as possible a measure of liquidity which at the same time is readily influenceable and linked to changes in the supply of bank loans. It may be added that, in order to make allowances for the upward trend in banking operations and in liquidity requirements, the liquidity measure is usually presented as a ratio to total deposits (sight, time and savings deposits, excluding funds with maturities of 4 years and over) by non-bank sectors and foreign banks.

---

10. In the new definition this component has become a positive item: "unused Lombard margin." It is only relevant as long as the Bundesbank is ready to grant credit of this type; since 1st June 1973 this has no longer been the case (cf. Appendix II, page 109 and Appendix III).

c) ACTIONS ON BANK LIQUIDITY

In its regular analysis—notably Table 1.3 "Bank Liquidity" published in its *Monthly Report*—the Bundesbank makes use of a distinction between "market" and "policy" factors among the sources of changes in liquidity. This distinction, which can hardly be made analytically rigorous,[11] leaves the following main influences in the category of market (or autonomous) factors:

 i) the net external balance, i.e. the change in the net foreign reserve assets of the Bundesbank plus the change in the banks' gross short-term foreign assets (money market paper and claims on banks) convertible into reserves at the Bundesbank; this has been the major factor in the supply of liquidity during the period under study;

 ii) changes in currency and deposits held with the Bundesbank by private non-banks, which has been the major liquidity-absorbing factor; and

 iii) changes in net government balances held at the Bundesbank and in the public authorities' money market indebtedness to the banking system. These changes have, on occasion, reflected deliberate debt management policies (see pages 51 and 55) and to that extent their classification as a "market" factor is debatable.

The task of the policy instruments, then, is to offset or reinforce the impact of the market factors in order to bring about the level of bank liquidity (and its ratio to deposits) considered to be consistent with the desired trend of bank lending. To this end the Bundesbank makes frequent use of two main instruments: changes in minimum reserve requirement ratios[12] and changes in rediscount quotas. It should be noted that, during most of the period under review, open market operations in money market paper were generally conducted with the banks (see page 37), and although they changed the composition of bank liquidity, they did not affect its total supply. On the other hand, money market operations with a selected group of non-bank institutions which were conducted at certain times, and operations in public authority bonds which took place between 1967 and 1969, did affect bank liquidity. Open market operations in money market paper with the general public which started in mid-1971 also strengthened the authorities' leverage on bank liquidity. Since the beginning of 1972, the Bardepot regulations have become an additional policy factor affecting bank liquidity.

It is conceivable that the change in interest rate structure which the traditional dealings in money market paper with the banks bring about may lead to a change in the banks' asset preference and in the relationship between bank liquidity and bank credit. The Bundesbank's swap operations do not change the volume of bank liquidity, but only its composition

---

11. It will not be retained in the form here outlined partly because of a different treatment of required reserves, partly because not all of the data relating to the present definition of bank liquidity are available prior to 1968.

12. In its regular analysis the Bundesbank includes among the policy factors the total change in required reserves. It does not distinguish between the effects of increases in deposits and changes in the minimum reserve ratios. The present study attempts to separate the two and to include the deposit-linked changes in required reserves among the market factors.

between domestic and foreign short-term assets (see page 38). However, they could also affect the banks' portfolio selection in the same way as do open market operations. Some instruments of interest rate policy, like changes in the discount rate and the Lombard rate, can also change the relationship between bank liquidity and credit by changing the cost of converting secondary liquid reserves into primary reserves.

III

THE USE OF MONETARY POLICY AND ITS IMPACT ON FINANCIAL VARIABLES

a) THE DATING OF POLICY PHASES AND THEIR CYCLICAL CONTEXT

The present Part describes briefly the cyclical context in which monetary policy was used, identifies the main policy phases and seeks to assess the impact on financial variables. There are three main ways in which policy phases may be identified:

i) by reversals in the use of major policy instruments;

ii) by observed changes in a certain financial variable assumed to indicate the stance of monetary policy; and

iii) by changes in a financial variable regarded as an approximate indicator of general monetary conditions.

These three ways give somewhat conflicting results in Germany, probably more so than elsewhere, because of the delicate and rapidly changing supply-demand balance domestically and the increasingly strong interaction during the period 1960-71 between national financial centres.

With the first method, it is possible to distinguish three basically restrictive and three expansionary or accommodating phases, each introduced by a reversal of one of the major policy instruments described in Part II (Table 8). But while the start of these phases is reasonably well identifiable as a signal of changing intentions (or evaluations) on the part

TABLE 8. DATING OF POLICY CHANGES

	by instrument changes	by liquidity ratio
First restrictive phase:		
Beginning	September 1959	September 1959
End......................	October 1960	October 1960
Second restrictive phase:		
Beginning	August 1964	July/August 1964
End......................	December 1966	June 1966
Third restrictive phase:		
Beginning	February 1969	January 1969
End......................	September 1971	March 1970

of the authorities, the characterisation loses precision some way into these periods, notably in the very long accommodating phase prior to the summer of 1964 and in the 1969-71 "restrictive" phase. Policy factors constitute only part of the influences on bank liquidity and interest rates, and measures primarily designed to offset the market factors operating on liquidity or foreign interest rate movements are, at most, indicative of an unchanged policy stance. "Policy" comprises not only what a central bank does, but also what it chooses not to do; depending on how financial market conditions are developing there may seem to be good reasons, at any one time, for the monetary authorities to do nothing, a little, or a lot. An analysis of changes in policy instruments is therefore mainly of descriptive value.

An alternative is to look at fluctuations in the bank liquidity ratio, the main operating target used by the Bundesbank, and identify policy phases by its major turning points (Chart 11). This method is still far short of being a reliable one. It assumes that changes in the bank liquidity ratio have reflected policy intentions closely, a view which can hardly be maintained in the light of the violent swings in some of the non-policy influences. Even if this assumption were nearly correct, one could not determine by looking only at observed changes in the bank liquidity ratio whether policy had become more or less restrictive. It would be necessary also to evaluate whether observed fluctuations in the liquidity ratio could actually be expected to exert a more or less expansionary impact on bank behaviour since the underlying causal relationships may be of a rather complex nature.

One might argue that the bank liquidity ratio is neither a dominant strategic variable nor an indicator of the stance of policy in cases where:

i) *individual* banks tend to adjust their lending policies to a broader measure of secondary liquidity that includes assets which though not directly convertible at the central bank into primary money, possess a high degree of "shiftability" (bankers' balances, first-rate commercial bills and securities in excess of individual banks' rediscount and Lombard quotas, etc.);

ii) the amount and composition of liquid assets that banks may voluntarily wish to hold against total deposits are undergoing long and short-term changes reflecting variations in bank asset preferences and portfolio behaviour. The interpretation of, say, a decline in the liquidity ratio as evidence of a tightening of policy may be misleading, if banks' demand for liquid assets has fallen even more—a situation which may have been brought about by changes in banks' risk evaluation and diversification policies, the existing and expected yield differentials between liquid assets and banks' other earning assets, the level of liquid reserves relative to past standards at which turning points occur, and expectations pertaining to "market factors" operating on bank liquidity and the course of monetary policy at home and abroad;

iii) observation periods are not very short. In this case, even under the assumption that the banks' asset preference does not change, causal links between changes in the liquidity ratio and bank lending behaviour are likely to be blurred; variations in the ratio cannot be regarded as purely determined by policy actions

Chart 11. BANK LIQUIDITY
SEASONALLY ADJUSTED

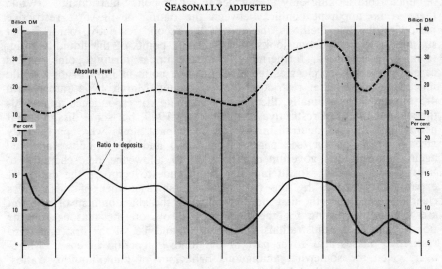

CHANGES IN MONETARY POLICY INSTRUMENTS

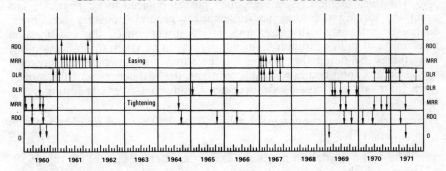

DLR = Discount and Lombard Rates;
MRR = Minimum Reserve Ratios;
RDQ = Rediscount Quotas;
O = Other.

on the level of bank liquidity, if banks have already been in the process of adjusting their portfolio to a pattern existing before policy actions.

Another candidate for the indicator of the stance of monetary policy would be short-term market rates. Because of the visually clear (inverse) relationship of the liquidity ratio and short-term interest rates, a roughly similar dating would be obtained by using major turning points in money market rates (Chart 17). Thus, despite the possible short-comings, changes in the liquidity ratio are the main method used in dating policy phases in the present Part. The restrictive phases that emerge from

45

inspection of Chart 11 are listed in Table 8 and compared with those obtained from looking only at changes in major policy instruments. While there is no apparent conflict between the dating of the first restrictive period by the two methods, the end of the second restrictive phase is put six months earlier, if one looks at the turning points of the liquidity ratio. It must be admitted, furthermore, that the upper turning point in this case is not nearly so clear as the lower turning point in June 1966; it could indeed be argued that restriction started around March 1964 rather than 4-5 months later. Finally, there is approximate correspondence as regards the start of the third restrictive phase in early 1969, but some disagreement about its end; the neutralising effects of capital flows were particularly strong in this period (see pages 53 and 64) and the liquidity ratio fell again following the government's decision to allow the deutschemark to float in May 1971. No attempt has been made to compare the dating of expansionary phases by the two methods, since neither of them gives clear results. Since the first months following the abandonment of restraint are usually interesting for the light they throw on the reasons for the policy change, the illustrations, in Charts 12 and 14, of the first and third restrictive phases also cover part of the following period of ease. Moreover, given the somewhat ambiguous behaviour of bank liquidity ratios, the end of the second and third restrictive periods has been dated in accordance with the turning of policy instrument changes.

The third method of dating policy phases referred to on page 41, viz. using the turning points as an indicator of general monetary conditions, cannot be adequately discussed prior to a discussion of the transmission mechanism of policy through financial markets to be taken up in Section (c). But it may be noted that dating by the three main monetary aggregates suggested, i.e. total domestic bank credit and the two concepts of the money stock (narrowly and broadly defined) gives somewhat divergent results.

First restrictive phase: September 1959-October 1960 and its abandonment (Chart 12)

The first episode summarised here is the attempt to cool off the 1959-61 boom which saw the first revaluation of the deutschemark. Demand pressures on German resources began to mount rapidly from the first quarter of 1959, with an extremely sharp upsurge in both foreign and domestic orders for manufactured goods. Unemployment was still at about 3 per cent at the beginning of the year, but declined rapidly thereafter—to less than $\frac{1}{2}$ per cent in early 1961. Pressure on costs and prices began to increase in the early summer of 1959.

Monetary restraint began in September 1959, i.e. about six months after the onset of the boom, with the raising of the discount rate; quantitative measures began to be taken in November.[1] They included a five-step tightening of minimum reserve requirements, raising the average required minimum reserve ratio from 8.1 to 12.6 per cent by August 1960; reductions in rediscount quotas; and some use of open market policy. Accompanying the Bundesbank's quantitative policy measures, the discount and Lombard rates were raised, in several stages, from 2.75 and 3.75 per

---

1. A cut in rediscount quotas in October 1959 was mainly of an administrative nature, but it did reduce quotas by about 20 per cent.

Chart 12. BANK LIQUIDITY DEVELOPMENTS: FIRST RESTRICTIVE PHASE[1]

Factors affecting bank liquidity[1]

Billion DM

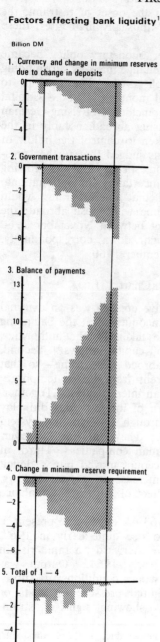

1. Currency and change in minimum reserves due to change in deposits

2. Government transactions

3. Balance of payments

4. Change in minimum reserve requirement

5. Total of 1 — 4

1959   1960   1961

Changes in bank liquidity and the liquidity ratio

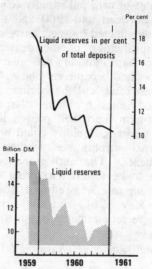

Per cent

Liquid reserves in per cent of total deposits

Billion DM

Liquid reserves

1959   1960   1961

Minimum reserve requirements began to be made more stringent in November 1959 and were further tightened, in four successive steps, through July 1960. Easing of reserve requirements began in December 1960. Cuts in rediscount quotas became effective in October 1959 and March and July 1960.

In the twelve months through September 1960, the volume of liquidity fell by about DM 9 billion or together with the liquidity ratio, by about half. About DM 6.5 billion of the decline through September resulted from growth in the money supply and in public authorities' net cash balances at the Bundesbank. Liquidity additions from external transactions appear to have been slightly higher; as shown in the Chart, the Bundesbank's net foreign assets increased by about DM 10 billion, of which about DM 2 billion reflected a run-down of the banks' short-term foreign assets. The increases in minimum reserve ratios absorbed about DM 4.5 billion. The effects of cuts in rediscount quotas and of open-market operations seem to have been somewhat more important. Through July, total rediscount quotas (used or unused) fell by about one-third, and the unused part fell by about one-half. Open-market operations in 1960 included sales to banks of "money market paper" not eligible for repurchase by the Bundesbank, except with prior agreement, within two years.

In the four months through January 1961, continued additions to bank liquidity from external transactions were only partly offset by the effects of money supply growth and the government's cash position. No further actions were taken by the Bundesbank, in line with the decision to bring German monetary conditions closer to those prevailing elsewhere.

1. Cumulative changes from the start of monetary restraint.

47

cent, respectively, in September 1959, to 5 and 6 per cent by June 1960. The banking system's liquid reserves, and the liquidity ratio, were halved in the thirteen months to September 1960.[2] At the onset of restraint, the money and credit aggregates had been rising at unusually high rates; these rates of growth fell rapidly (Chart 17).

Between mid-1960 and mid-1961, however, monetary policy became heavily affected by speculative disturbances in exchange markets surrounding the revaluation of the deutschemark in March 1961. The attempt to reduce bank liquidity was abandoned in the final months of 1960. Capital inflows had become very large, attracted by the coincidence of rising German interest rates and the beginning of monetary easing abroad, notably in the United States; a number of special measures taken to control the inflow of short-term funds had proven insufficient. It was judged that further pressure on bank liquidity could be self-defeating domestically, and the growing external surplus was leading to increasing uncertainty in international payments. The authorities became convinced that interest rates would have to be lowered to bring them more into line with those abroad; the discount rate was reduced from 5 to 3 per cent between November 1960 and May 1961, and the Lombard rate brought down correspondingly. Reserve requirements began to be eased in December 1960.

Second restrictive phase: mid-1964 to end-1966 (Chart 13)

A major feature of the mid-1960's restrictive episode was an external environment substantially different from those encountered at the beginning and the end of the decade. First, steps were taken by the authorities, before the onset of domestic restraint, to ward off capital inflows.[3] Second, throughout most of the period, interest rates abroad were rising—so that the Bundesbank felt freer (although, as apparent from its contemporary comment, not completely free) to push up German interest rates. Together, the measures taken and the international pattern of interest rates did play some role in keeping down capital inflows through the banking system and through the bond market in this period. They did not, however, prevent recourse to borrowing abroad by German companies. Third, at the height of the boom, the current external account moved into a deficit that was more than sufficient to offset the increase in capital inflows. As a result, through much of the period, the effect of the external balance was to drain liquidity from the banking system.

Indicators of the early course of the 1963-64 expansion present a rather mixed picture. Export orders began to rise quite early in 1963, and domestic orders for capital goods very soon afterwards; a rapid rise in permits granted for housebuilding began in early 1964. Output was depressed in early 1963, reflecting very severe winter conditions; its subsequent sharp recovery occurred without any initial pressure on costs or prices. But by mid-1964, the economy was showing signs of strain.

---

2. This reduction in the liquidity ratio was the net product of the Bundesbank's restrictive measures, liquidity additions from the external surplus, and the growth of the money supply (see Chart 12 and the note therewith).

3. One of these—the Withholding Tax on interest payable to foreigners on German fixed-interest securities—became effective only in March 1965, but its announcement in March 1964 led immediately to a sharp fall in foreign purchases of German bonds.

48

Chart 13. BANK LIQUIDITY DEVELOPMENTS:
SECOND RESTRICTIVE PHASE

Factors affecting bank liquidity
Billion DM

1. Currency and change in minimum reserves due to change in deposits

2. Government transactions

3. Balance of payments

4. Miscellaneous

5. Total of 1 — 4

6. Change in minimum reserve requirements

7. Total of 5 — 6

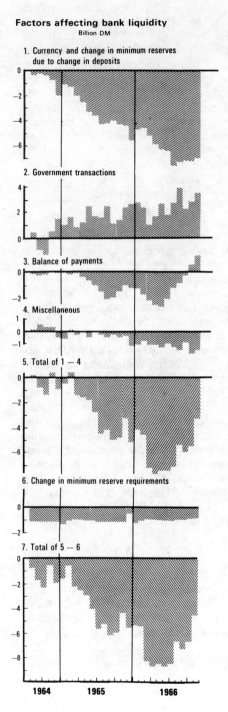

Changes in bank liquidity and the liquidity ratio
Per cent

Liquid reserves in per cent of total deposits

Billion DM

Liquid reserves

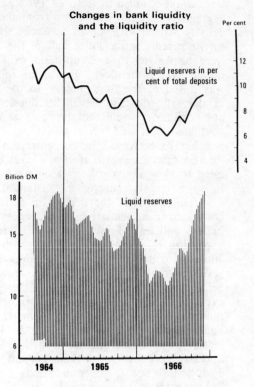

Minimum reserve requirements on domestic deposits were raised in August 1964. Rediscount quotas were cut in the same month, and again in October 1965 and in May 1966. The volume of bank liquidity declined by DM 7 billion in the two years through June 1966 and the liquidity ratio fell from 12 to under 5 per cent. The increase in the money supply and an external deficit absorbed somewhat over DM 8 billion; a net cash deficit of the public authorities supplied about DM 2 billion; open-market sales and an increase in minimum reserve ratios appear to have mopped-up about DM 1 billion; and it would seem that the cuts in rediscount quotas kept them about in line with their underlying growth.

49

Measures of domestic monetary restraint began to be taken with the raising of required reserve ratios in August 1964. Bank liquidity had already come under pressure earlier in the year, largely as a result of the defensive external measures described above,[4] and from March 1964 the bank liquidity ratio declined almost continuously. Rediscount quotas were again reduced in October 1965. The growth of the money and credit aggregates began to slow down from about the middle of 1965 and economic activity started to level off at about the same time. But prices continued to rise rapidly in the latter half of the year and in early 1966—when there were also signs of a resumption of the growth of demand. Rediscount quotas were, therefore, cut again in May 1966 and the discount rate was raised at the same time. In the second half of the year the growth of domestic demand began to decelerate rather rapidly. The monetary authorities were reluctant to reverse monetary policy quickly, because of continued cost and price pressures. They did allow the bank liquidity position to be eased by an emergent balance of payments surplus, and interest rates began to decline. But the expansion of bank credit continued to slow down though the year, and in the bond market the decline in yields largely reflected a substantial fall in new issues.

The extent of the decline in activity in the second half of 1966 was considerably accentuated by fiscal developments. In 1965 the effects of budget policies followed by the Federal and Länder authorities had been expansionary, partly reflecting tax cuts at the beginning of that year; this stimulus to activity began to decline quite early in 1966. Later in 1966 revenue receipts by all levels of government began to fall substantially below budget estimates, because the growth of income was weaker than expected. But government expenditures were also cut back, so that fiscal policy failed to provide any automatic stabilisation. The expenditure cutbacks partly reflected reluctance to borrow; many local authorities are legally prohibited from allowing their debt servicing obligations to exceed a certain proportion of their current revenues. In the latter months of 1966 unfavourable revenue trends coincided with (to that date) record interest rates in the bond market: in mid-1966 general agreement was reached among public authorities that efforts should be made to abstain from the bond market until interest rates had been reduced. Expenditure cuts fell both on public authorities' own investment and on government assistance to housing. Orders in connection with civil engineering projects placed by the local authorities in 1966 were 18 per cent lower than in 1965. By the end of 1966 expert opinion in Germany had increasingly become aware of the imminent danger of undesirable recessionary developments, which rapidly gained momentum soon after.

Third restrictive phase: early 1969-September 1971 and its abandonment
   (Chart 14)

From mid-1968 the recovery from the previous recession was fully assured, with both foreign and domestic demand rising rapidly. Consideration began to be given to the need for a more restrictive policy stance. But the large external surplus on current account and interest rate devel-

---

4. A cut in rediscount quotas in September 1964 was also aimed at discouraging capital inflows—see Appendix III, Chronology.

opments abroad posed a risk of substantial capital inflows, for arbitrage and speculative reasons, if monetary conditions were to be tightened. For this reason, the Bundesbank in complete privacy began to advocate a revaluation of the deutschemark in the summer of 1968. At the time, however, this was not acceptable to the government authorities although the necessity for external corrective measures became progressively apparent. Despite the quick revival in activity, the trade surplus assumed discomforting proportions during 1968, and public discussion of a change in parity and revaluation rumours led to massive inflows of capital in the closing months of the year. In November special tax measures were taken to affect the trade balance; these were widely regarded as but a temporary and insufficient "revaluation substitute".

In any event, the evidence of the early months of 1969 did not suggest that the fiscal measures taken were likely to slow down the pace of demand with sufficient speed. Meanwhile, interest rates abroad had begun to rise, reducing the constraints felt on monetary policy. A first step towards tightening was the cessation of open market purchases of long-term securities in February. The Lombard rate was raised in March and again in April together with an increase in the discount rate. Discreet quantitative measures began in June, with the raising of minimum reserve requirements;[5] in July, a cut in rediscount quotas (decided in March) became effective, and refunding of short-term government debt made an important contribution to the reduction of bank liquidity. But during the summer months the predominant influence on bank liquidity and money market conditions was the ebb and flow of speculative capital movements.

The deutschemark was revalued in October 1969 by 9.3 per cent following a brief period of floating. In the next few months there were massive capital outflows and a very substantial fall in the volume of the banks' liquid reserves. By the end of the year the liquidity ratio had fallen to mid-1966 levels, and the Bundesbank temporarily eased its minimum reserve requirements. Nevertheless, the liquidity ratio continued to fall, reaching in March 1970 its lowest level (less than 6 per cent) during the period under review. The development of interest rates rather closely mirrored that of bank liquidity. Money market rates rose steeply from around the middle of 1969 and reached a peak in May 1970.

In the course of the first half of 1970 it became increasingly clear that the German economy was cooling off less quickly than had been expected immediately following the revaluation. Export orders for manufactured goods had flattened out from the time of the October 1969 revaluation, and inventory accumulation as well as indicators of business expectations showed a weaker picture; but overall activity remained unexpectedly strong, while price and wage developments showed no sign of moderation. In these circumstances further restrictive policy steps seemed to be justified—reserve requirements were raised, rediscount quotas were cut again and open market policy remained restrictive. But in the end these actions did not keep pace with the expansionary effects of short-term capital inflows mainly in the form of interest-induced borrowing abroad

---

5. 100 per cent reserve requirements on additions to liabilities to non-residents, introduced in December 1968 and maintained, with modifications, through October 1969, were aimed at deterring speculative capital inflows or encouraging reflows of speculative funds.

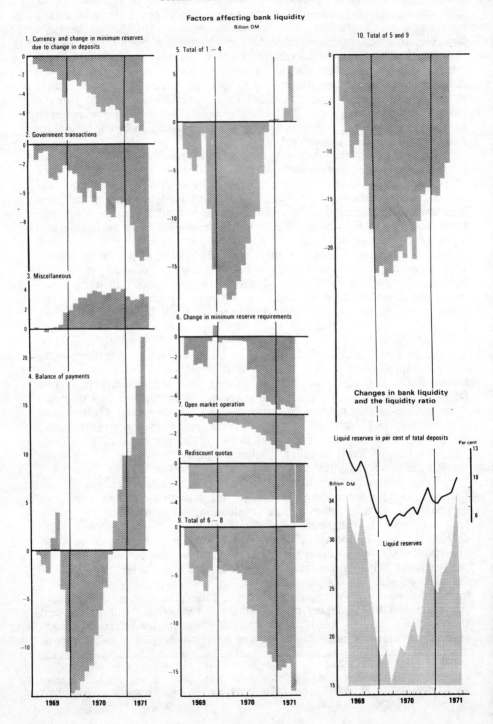

Chart 14. BANK LIQUIDITY DEVELOPMENTS: THIRD RESTRICTIVE PHASE

Factors affecting bank liquidity
Billion DM

1. Currency and change in minimum reserves due to change in deposits

2. Government transactions

3. Miscellaneous

4. Balance of payments

5. Total of 1 — 4

6. Change in minimum reserve requirements

7. Open market operation

8. Rediscount quotas

9. Total of 6 — 8

10. Total of 5 and 9

Changes in bank liquidity and the liquidity ratio

Liquid reserves in per cent of total deposits

Per cent

Billion DM

Liquid reserves

1969   1970   1971

52

by German companies, and the liquidity ratio edged upwards. Again the changing trend in liquidity was reflected in interest rates; the Bundesbank lowered discount and Lombard rates in July to stem the inflow of short-term capital while maintaining some quantitative pressure through an increase in incremental reserve requirements on non-resident liabilities, which became effective in September.

There was a brief interval between the late autumn of 1970 and the spring of 1971 when monetary policy could be said to have been easing on the evidence of both changes in policy instruments and the development of the liquidity ratio. A severe profit squeeze, the weakening of foreign demand and tighter monetary and fiscal policies (including a renewal of fiscal restraint in May and July 1970) dampened the growth of demand and output in the second half of 1970. Between November and April Bundesbank lending rates were lowered in three steps; but the reduction of official interest rates in April was accompanied by a curtailment of the banks' rediscount quotas as the authorities saw no justification for further monetary relaxation on domestic grounds. Indeed, there was an unexpectedly strong revival of activity in the first few months of 1971, while prices and wages continued to rise rapidly. However, large inflows of short-term funds responding to international interest rate differentials and growing uneasiness in foreign exchange markets prevented the central bank from effectively gaining control over monetary aggregates. In early May, a speculative upheaval led to the government's decision to permit the deutschemark to float; this gave more freedom of manoeuvre to the central bank. The reversal of capital flows and an increase in minimum reserve requirements in June caused a fall in the liquidity ratio[6] and market interest rates edged up again. By the autumn of 1971 the economy showed definite signs of cooling off, and continued unexpected upward pressure on the deutschemark underlined the need for a relaxation of the monetary reins.

First phase of easing: November 1960 onwards (Chart 15)

Of the three periods of easing, or easy monetary policy, the earliest and longest is the most difficult to characterise. After the initial exter-

---

6. This takes no account of the fact that banks' short-term foreign assets lost their high degree of "moneyness" during the floating period, since the central bank's commitment to support the spot rate had been suspended.

NOTES OF CHART 14

Minimum reserve ratios on domestic liabilities were raised in June and August 1969, were briefly reduced later that year, and were raised further, in three eps, during 1970. There were cuts in rediscount quotas in 1969, 1970, and early 1971. Over the two years through May 1971 government transactions and the increase the money supply absorbed about DM 21 billion of liquidity, while the underlying growth of rediscount quotas and other miscellaneous influences supplied about M 3 billion; the tightening of minimum reserve requirements, open market operations and cuts in rediscount quotas similarly absorbed about 18 billion. But for most the period, the dominant influence was the balance of payment. In the four months following the revaluation of the deutschemark in October 1969, there were massive apital outflows which induced the easing of reserve requirements at the end of 1969. But net capital inflows began to ensue early in 1970; with the monetary easing foreign markets at mid-year, they began to accelerate. In the sixteen months through May 1971, transactions on external account supplied no less than DM 45 billion.

In the first fifteen months of restriction, both the volume of liquidity and the ratio to deposits declined by about half. But from then until the floating of the eutschemark in May 1971, there was an almost continual increase. The volume returned to about pre-restriction levels, and the liquidity ratio rose to slightly above) per cent.

53

Chart 15. BANK LIQUIDITY DEVELOPMENTS:
FIRST PHASE OF EASING

Factors affecting bank liquidity
Billion DM

Changes in bank liquidity and the liquidity ratio

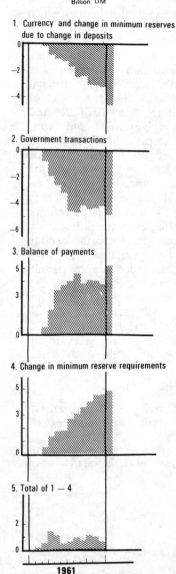

1. Currency and change in minimum reserves due to change in deposits

2. Government transactions

3. Balance of payments

4. Change in minimum reserve requirements

5. Total of 1 — 4

1961

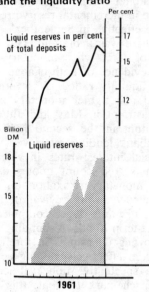

Reserve requirements began to be eased in February 1961. There were reductions in all subsequent months through December, except in May and November. Rediscount quotas were restored in November to their levels of October 1959. Open market policy included the freeing of the money market paper originally sold to the banks in 1960 for a period of two years. In the eleven months through December, the liquidity volume returned approximately to the mid-1959 level, and the ratio rose from 10 to 15 per cent. External transactions continued to boost liquidity to an even greater extent than shown in the Chart, since the banks now rebuilt their short-term foreign assets. The effect of the balance of payments was outweighed by the combined influences of a rising money supply and a continued increase in government cash balances at the Bundesbank. Decreases in minimum reserve requirements supplied about DM 5 billion. The total effect of open market operations and changes in rediscount quotas seems to have been of the same order.

nally inspired adjustments of interest rates and of minimum reserve requirements, mentioned on page 46 above, had been made, there followed a long period of more than two years during which the stance of policy does not suggest that the authorities were anxious to modify the course of the economy. Apart from a very gradual upward adjustment of the

Bundesbank's selling rates on the money market, no changes in monetary instruments were made; the liquidity ratio fluctuated within a narrow band. This basically accommodating stance was explained by the smoothness of developments in most indicators between early 1962 and early 1964; both external and domestic demand expanded steadily—the latter at a slightly lower rate than during the preceding three years—the current account remained near equilibrium and price increases were moderate.

Second phase of easing: end-1966 onwards (Chart 16)

This was a period of active easing, during the early months of which the authorities were greatly concerned about the sluggishness of domestic demand. By the turn of the year 1966, almost all components of domestic expenditure were falling, and the flow of orders and other indicators suggested that further declines were to be expected. Moreover, some abatement had occurred in cost and price increases. In these circumstances, monetary policy was rapidly eased towards the end of 1966. Fiscal policy also aimed at giving a substantial impulse to the economy—and, as noted earlier, in this period debt management began to play a more important role in German economic policy.

The Bundesbank discount rate was reduced from 5 to 3 per cent in four steps between January and May 1967, and the reserve ratios were reduced in several stages: the effective average ratio fell from 8.0 to 5.3 per cent, or by about one-third, between January and September. There was a sharp shift in the structure of Federal and Länder debt towards shorter-term forms, thus increasing the supply of assets available in liquid form to the banks. Moreover, during the summer months certain medium-term bonds of the Federal and Länder governments with a remaining life of not longer than 18 months were made eligible for purchase by the Bundesbank in its money market operations, so that these too could be regarded as liquid assets by the banking system.

The problems of the monetary authorities in stimulating the economy in 1967 were somewhat aggravated by external developments, though less severely than in the restrictive phases examined in this paper. The banks responded to a release of minimum reserve balances by increasing their short-term foreign assets rather than domestic lending and portfolio investments. This reflected interest differentials in favour of foreign countries and weak demand for funds by domestic enterprises in line with the delayed pick-up in real activity. Higher interest rates abroad and liquid financial positions of non-bank sectors also encouraged long-term capital flows. Indeed, 1967 was the first year in the decade when Germany became a net exporter of private long-term capital. The strong external current account more than offset the effects of the capital outflow on bank liquidity, but expectational effects set up by the outward movement of funds (particularly large purchases of foreign bonds by German banks) retarded the downward movement of long-term interest rates. Furthermore, market sentiments seem to have been adversely affected by public reactions to the first experience of deficit budgeting in Germany in the post-war period. The decline in long-term interest rates was interrupted at midyear. In August, the Bundesbank began, for the first time, open market operations in long-term bonds. Long-term interest rates did fall further thereafter, but only very gradually.

Chart 16. BANK LIQUIDITY DEVELOPMENTS:
SECOND PHASE OF EASING

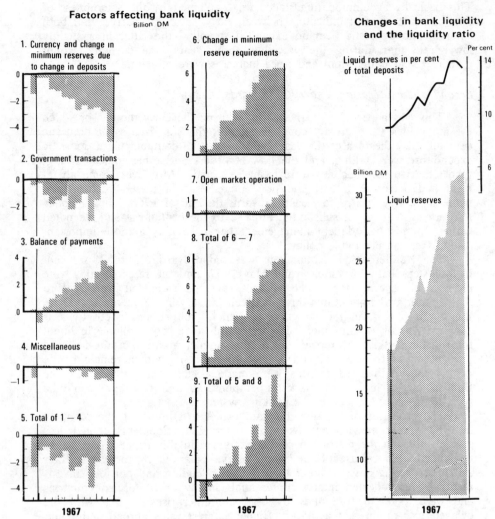

Factors affecting bank liquidity
Billion DM

1. Currency and change in minimum reserves due to change in deposits

2. Government transactions

3. Balance of payments

4. Miscellaneous

5. Total of 1 — 4

6. Change in minimum reserve requirements

7. Open market operation

8. Total of 6 — 7

9. Total of 5 and 8

1967

Changes in bank liquidity and the liquidity ratio
Per cent

Liquid reserves in per cent of total deposits

Billion DM

Liquid reserves

1967

Minimum reserve requirements began to be eased in December 1966. There were five further easings through September 1967. The volume of liquidity rose by about DM 13 billion during the twelve months ending in December, the ratio rose from 9 to nearly 14 per cent. The increase in the money supply absorbed about DM 5 billion, and external transactions provided about DM 3,5 billion. Over the whole period, there was little net effect from government cash transactions, but sales of money market paper by public authorities supplied about DM 4,5 billion in the calendar year 1967. (Monthly details are not available). The reductions in minimum reserve requirements supplied about DM 6,5 billion, and open market operations (which became more active at the end of the year) supplied about DM 1.5 billion. There was also some underlying growth of rediscount quotas.

The external surplus and the policy measures combined to increase the liquidity ratio from 9 to 14 per cent in the course of 1967 (Chart 11). It subsequently stabilised at around this level as active policy measures petered out; the next measures taken were those at the end of the following year (1968), when capital flows into Germany were again becoming a matter of concern after the unrest in European currency markets throughout the summer and autumn of 1968. By that time the upswing in real demand had in any case become very obvious.

Third phase of easing: October 1971 to early 1972

The easing which took place between October 1971 and February 1972 included three reductions in official lending rates and a lowering, in two steps, of minimum reserve ratios. It constituted but a short-lived interlude before the Bundesbank adopted a new decidedly restrictive policy posture around, perhaps, mid-1972.[7] The timing of the central bank's measures was heavily influenced by the need to prevent an unwanted appreciation of the floating deutschemark and the necessity to support the new DM central rate, established under the Smithsonian agreement. Although demand pressures were subsiding markedly in the second half of 1971 and the floating of the deutschemark had exerted some moderating influence on wage and price behaviour, the dampening of inflationary expectations and cost pressures was far from complete. With a new upswing getting under way around the turn of the year at relatively high levels of resource utilisation, the authorities saw little justification for continuing a policy of active easing in early 1972.

b) THE PROBLEM OF CAPITAL FLOWS: SOME GENERAL EXPERIENCE FROM POLICY PHASES

The review of experience in the three restrictive and three expansionary ("easing") policy phases indicates how strongly the German monetary authorities have found their efforts to design a monetary policy appropriate from a domestic viewpoint undermined by capital flows. The problem was particularly acute in the first and third restrictive phases, and in both cases it led to basic modifications of policy; but it also arose in the period of easing during much of 1967. The present section is devoted to a review of the changing extent to which such flows offset the Bundesbank's restrictive policy moves, and seeks tentatively to evaluate the effectiveness of special measures adopted by the authorities to ward off undesirable short-term inflows. Capital flows change both the domestic liquidity and the international reserves of a country; in the present section only the former effect is discussed, the question of the desirability of the change in international reserves being left for brief comment in Part V.

The *types of capital flows* causing major problems (Table 9) and the authorities' *offsetting measures* (Table 10) have varied. During the first restrictive phase in 1960, one important item was an inflow of foreign portfolio funds. The inflow of bank funds was also important in 1960; so also was a relatively large positive balancing item in the balance of payments which largely reflected leads and lags in payments for current transactions or other unrecorded credit from abroad received by German enterprises. While these disequilibrating inflows could to some extent be attri-

---

7. Towards the end of the period under study, identification of policy phases according to turning points in the liquidity ratio has become rather difficult since the floating of the deutschemark temporarily reduced the "moneyness" of banks' short-term foreign assets, and movements in the ratio have, in any case, been rather small and somewhat erratic.

TABLE 9. PRIVATE CAPITAL MOVEMENTS AFFECTING BANK LIQUIDITY
DM BILLION

	1960	1969	1970	First 5 months	
				1970	1971
1. *Long-term capital, net*	*1.14*	*-21.23*	*-0.49*	*-4.16*	*2.13*
1.1. Increase (-) in German assets	-1.39	-22.00	-7.90	-4.33	-1.46
of which:					
1.1.1. Portfolio capital	-0.52	-9.51	-2.02	-1.17	-0.36
1.1.2. Bank lending	0.03	-9.41	-2.43	-1.72	0.28
1.2. Increase in German liabilities	2.53	0.77	7.39	0.18	3.59
of which:					
1.2.1. Portfolio capital	1.64	-1.21	1.34	0.17	0.75
2. *Short-term capital, net*[1]	*1.74*	*6.74*	*14.28*	*3.36*	*6.70*
2.1. Commercial banks' liabilities	1.15	6.97	7.83	1.29	-0.89
2.2. Enterprises' recorded assets and liabilities, net	0.59	-0.24	6.45	2.07	7.59
3. *Errors and omissions in the balance of payments*	*1.74*	*2.52*	*8.23*	*3.66*	*12.23*
4. TOTAL ABOVE	4.63	-11.97	22.02	2.86	21.06
Memorandum items:					
5.1. Banks' short-term foreign assets (increase -)	1.22	-2.65	0.09	-0.05	-3.10
5.2. Total capital	3.53	-16.49	19.24	1.74	18.28

1. Excluding banks' short-term foreign assets, largely comprising assets included in bank liquidity; see Line 5.1.
Source : Deutsche Bundesbank.

buted to the growing discrepancy between interest rate movements at home and abroad (Charts 17 and 18), speculative disturbances in exchange markets seem to have played a dominant role immediately following the package of restrictive measures that the Bundesbank introduced in mid-1960. The accompanying restrictions on interest payments on non-resident deposits and money market investments by foreigners (Table 10) should have mitigated short-term inflows into the banking system; however, accelerating purchases by non-residents of domestic securities and German enterprises' short-term foreign liabilities during 1960 suggest that speculation was diverted into unblocked financial channels rather than effectively warded off. Moreover, uncontrolled speculative inflows were unexpectedly enduring, since speculative pressures persisted until well after the revaluation of the deutschemark in March 1961 and obliged the Bundesbank to reverse its restrictive policy posture on external grounds.

During the second restrictive phase (1964-66), when a current account deficit contributed to the absence of speculative disturbances and interest rate developments abroad remained more conducive to the pursuit of restrictive monetary policies in Germany (see page 48), the authorities seem to have been reasonably successful in controlling capital inflows. Following the announcement of the Withholding Tax and the introduction of protective measures against foreign borrowing by the banking sector at the beginning of the period (Table 10), inflows of foreign portfolio capital and short-term banking funds were seldom in evidence during this phase. Recorded short-term foreign borrowing by the company sector rose significantly only towards the end of the period in response to the progressive tightening of domestic monetary conditions, while the emergence of a large positive errors and omissions item in the balance of payments during 1964-65 may have been connected with the marked deterioration of the trade balance.

During the third restrictive period starting in early 1969, inflows of foreign portfolio capital were recorded again—but on a smaller scale than in 1960. Much more important were:

— a large build-up of banks' short-term foreign liabilities (DM 7 billion in 1969 and DM 8 billion in 1970);
— a swing from approximate balance to a large inflow of recorded net short-term borrowing abroad by enterprises (DM 6.5 billion in 1970 and DM 7.5 billion in the first five months of 1971);
— an even greater change in the balancing item (a surplus of DM 8 billion for 1970 and DM 12 billion in the first five months of 1971).

Although during most of the period short-term capital flows were again heavily influenced by exchange-rate speculation and, in the first half of 1970, by a decline in international interest rates which coincided with tightening monetary conditions in Germany, the authorities seem to have had some success in containing short-term inflows through the banking system (Table 10).[8] However, short-term foreign borrowing by the com-

---

8. The bulk of the banking flows in 1969 was recorded after the 1969 revaluation when restrictions had been removed. Large inflows in the second half of 1970 seem to have been mainly related to holdings of DM deposits by foreign banks and monetary authorities not originating from the initiative of German banks and to interest arbitrage transactions in which foreign liabilities, which had been reinvested in short-term foreign assets, were exempted from minimum reserve requirements. Under these arrangements, banks' money market investments abroad were probably effectively "locked in", and indeed, in both 1970 and 1971, they did not significantly fluctuate.

TABLE 10. SPECIAL MEASURES AGAINST CAPITAL

FIRST EPISODE

January 1960:

Incremental reserve requirement ratios on non-resident deposits raised to legal maximum.

June 1960:

Interest payment on non-resident sight and time deposits and sale of domestic money market paper to non-residents (including repurchase agreements involving domestic bonds) prohibited; domestic bank guarantees on non-bank foreign liabilities subjected to licensing.

July 1960:

Exemption from minimum reserve requirements of foreign currency liabilities employed in foreign deposits and money market investments abroad abandoned.

SECOND EPISODE

February 1964:

Gentleman's agreement between domestic issuing consortium and government authorities aiming at reduced allotment of new issues of public bonds to non-resident buyers.

March 1964:

Interest payment on non-resident time deposits restricted (restrictions on interest payment on foreign demand deposits and sale of domestic money market paper to non-residents carried forward from June 1960).

March 1964:

Announcement of introduction of Withholding Tax on interest payable to non-residents on domestic fixed-interest securities.

April 1964:

Minimum reserve requirement ratios on non-resident deposits raised to legal maximum.

September 1964:

Reduction of banks' rediscount quotas corresponding to increase against end-January to end-June 1964 average of outstanding liabilities resulting from foreign borrowing by domestic banks.

pany sector, both recorded and unrecorded, rose to an unprecedented level; such flows had not been subject to controls before restrictive monetary policies were abandoned in the autumn of 1971. Also in 1970 and early 1971 there was a sharp reduction in the outflow of German long-term capital. An important element was a delayed slowdown in the accumulation by German banks of long-term assets abroad, in the form of security holdings and loans. Before the 1969 revaluation, banks had committed themselves heavily to their foreign clients, so that their lending activity abroad did not immediately react to the post-revaluation drain on

March 1965:

Withholding Tax announced in March 1964 put into effect.

THIRD EPISODE

November 1968-February 1969:

Acceptance of foreign deposits and foreign borrowing by German banks subjected to licensing.

December 1968-October 1969:

Incremental reserve requirement ratios on non-resident deposits raised to 100 per cent.

Early 1969-December 1969:

Restrictions on interest payment on foreign deposits and sale of domestic money market paper to non-residents carried forward.

August 1969-December 1969:

Exemption from minimum reserve requirements of foreign liabilities resulting from interest arbitrage restricted.

April 1970:

Incremental reserve requirement ratios on non-resident deposits re-introduced.

June 1970:

Banks' rediscount quotas reduced, corresponding to the increase against end-March 1970 in banks' foreign liabilities resulting from repurchase agreements and foreign discounting of commercial bills.

October 1970:

Exemption from minimum reserve requirements of foreign liabilities resulting from interest arbitrage restricted.

May 1971:

Restrictions on interest payment on foreign deposits (covering for the first time savings deposits exceeding DM 50,000) and sale of domestic money market paper to non-residents reintroduced.

bank liquidity. Moreover, there is some evidence that banks managed partly to evade existing disincentives and restrictions on short-term foreign borrowing by raising longer-term loans not covered by the special measures adopted. At the end of the third restrictive period the German authorities devised a new instrument of monetary policy to dampen future borrowing abroad by German enterprises and to restrict the raising of longer-term loans abroad by the banking system. In December 1971, legislation came into force empowering the government authorities and the Bundesbank, acting together, to require companies and credit institutions

Chart 17. INTEREST RATES AND MONETARY AGGREGATES

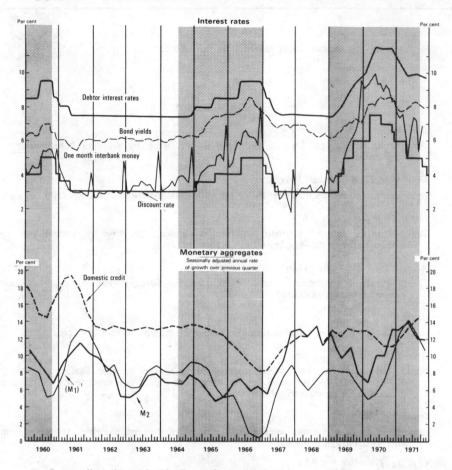

1. Seasonally adjusted by the Deutsche Bundesbank.

to maintain compulsory non-interest-bearing deposits ("Bardepots") with the Bundesbank against foreign financial credits. The maximum deposit rate that can be required was 50 per cent (100 per cent as from 22nd February 1973) of the credit liabilities incurred, the first DM 50,000 being exempted. Discussion of the draft legislation—particularly about the degree of proposed retroactivity—and uncertainty about the maturity of credits likely to be covered led to a substantial decline in German enterprises' short-term foreign indebtedness in the latter half of 1971—a time when speculative considerations had not completely disappeared. But at the same time there was an increase in the inflow of long-term funds borrowed abroad, possibly indicating that some short-term indebtedness was consolidated rather than repaid.

As regards the first restrictive phase, it is only possible, partly because of statistical difficulties, to give a rough idea of the *quantitative effect of*

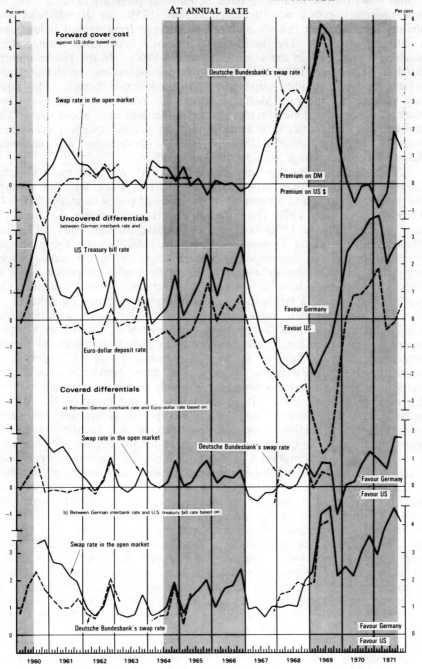

Chart 18. 3-MONTH INTEREST ARBITRAGE
AT ANNUAL RATE

1. Bundesbank's swap facilities were available for banks' money market investments abroad up to the spring of 1963 and from November 1968 until September 1969, only for the acquisition of U.S. Treasury bills between March 1964 and the spring of 1965, and for all types of financial investments abroad between November 1967 and November 1968.

capital flows on the volume of bank liquidity as presently defined. At the time monetary policy was tightened in late 1959, the Bundesbank was already recording net inflows of foreign exchange from capital inflows *and* a current surplus. The build-up of reserves accelerated immediately, reaching a peak rate in the second quarter of 1960. In the twelve months through September 1960 they were roughly equivalent to half of the volume of bank liquidity outstanding when restriction began. The liquidity volume and the ratio declined during this period—but for every two marks absorbed by policy factors the net effect was only about one. The problem became particularly acute during the second quarter; even then, however, some reduction (DM 0.4 billion) of liquidity was achieved, despite foreign exchange receipts (DM 3.6 billion).

Experience during the early months of 1970 was even more striking. Large inflows more than offset the absorption of bank liquidity through the domestic market and a comprehensive series of policy factors (Chart 14). Through December 1970 the external effects were nearly $1\frac{1}{2}$ times as large as the January 1970 volume of liquidity; through May 1971, the effects were more than $2\frac{1}{2}$ times as large, the liquidity ratio rising sharply over this period. It appeared not only that policy factors tended to be completely swamped by inflows, but that a tightening of policy could in some circumstances have a "perverse" effect on domestic liquidity by actually encouraging a larger inflow than originally absorbed by policy.

The unprecedented degree to which the restrictive monetary policy was counteracted in 1970-71 by short-term borrowing abroad by German companies may not have been solely due to powerful ephemeral factors influencing the direction of mobile international funds in a period of international monetary crisis; it may also have mirrored more lasting changes in the external environment in which domestic monetary policies are now being conducted. It is true that, during most of the period, exchange-rate expectations favoured an increase in companies' uncovered foreign currency liabilities and a swing into surplus of the errors and omissions item in the balance of payments under the impact of speculative leads and lags in international payments. While an immediate "perverse" reaction of speculative inflows in response to the reinforcement of monetary restraint had already been experienced in the first restrictive period, there was little evidence of speculation in the first half of 1970 to which the frustration of restrictive policy measures could have been attributed. From about mid-1970 onwards, when domestic interest rates began to be brought into line with international trends, a substantial part of companies' short-term financial borrowing abroad was denominated in deutschemarks. There was also a continuing strong financial incentive for non-speculative Euro-currency borrowing by German companies, since speculation in exchange markets depressed the forward dollar to abnormally low levels and reduced both the forward covering cost of borrowing in foreign currencies and, through interest arbitrage mechanisms, the interest cost of Euro-DM credits. It would thus appear that a major factor contributing to large-scale financial borrowing abroad by German companies has been the rapidly growing integration of the domestic credit system into international financial markets. While in earlier restrictive periods, and even at the beginning of the last boom, short-term borrowing abroad seemed to be restricted to a limited number of large domestic enterprises and multinational firms, smaller firms later followed their example,[9] assisted probably by domestic bank intermediation. Indeed, given the close relationships between individual banks and companies in Germany, it seems possible that some enterprise borrowing abroad was urged on the borrowers by banks, the aim of the latter being the improvement of their own individual liquidity positions. It is quite conceivable that, with growing links in recent years between the German financial system and the rapidly expanding Euro-money market, Bundesbank measures produced immediate credit rationing effects inducing domestic borrowers (and their banks) to turn abroad; indeed, econometric evidence suggests that capital inflows may systematically have offset the restrictive impact of the central bank's major policy instruments on banks' "free liquid reserves".[10]

Given the substantive changes in recent years in institutional factors bearing on the direction and volume of international financial flows in Germany, it is difficult to draw any general conclusions covering the three periods here under study. However, some of the policy experience seems to be important enough—and to have sufficient bearing on the future—to be summarised at this stage of the present review:

i) The authorities seem to have been relatively successful in controlling short-term foreign liabilities of the domestic banking system during most of the period. While, up to the late 1960's, such selective controls are likely to have had an overall dampening impact on short-term inflows in normal exchange market conditions, strong revaluation expectations in 1960-61 and 1969 appear to have undermined the authorities' protective measures, as speculative influences were diverted from banking to non-bank sector capital flows.

ii) In periods of heavy revaluation speculation, effective control of the "free liquid reserves" of the banking system was more or less frustrated, and there is some evidence that, at times, restrictive policy moves may even have contributed to an acceleration of speculative inflows. Given the large positive swings in these

---

9. In 1970 the recorded inflow of short-term company credits was based on statistics reported by about 1,000 firms. By May 1971, the number reporting had risen to about 1,300, and the number of wholly resident-owned and smaller enterprises involved rose substantially from the beginning of 1970. Revisions in the reporting requirements in mid-1971 brought the number reporting up to 3,300, and no doubt there was unreported foreign indebtedness during most of the period.

10. Domestic credit rationing effects as a cause of short-term inflows are mainly seen in recent econometric studies as coming through the errors and omissions item in response to changes in minimum reserve ratios. An additional incentive for short-term inflows was found to have resulted from the impact of monetary policy measures on domestic money market rates. A study by Michael G. Porter ("Capital Flows as an Offset to Monetary Policy: The German Experience", *International Monetary Fund Staff Papers*, July 1972) and by P. Kouri and M. Porter ("International Capital Flows and Portfolio Equilibrium", *unpublished* 1972) suggest that (*i*) a one percentage-point change in interest rates in favour of Germany leads to an inflow of about DM 5 billion within six months, (*ii*) the impact of the reserve requirement change is offset to the extent of 80-85 per cent by capital inflows within the same month. (Permission from the authors to refer to the studies is gratefully acknowledged). Similar evidence is provided in a recent German study in which changes in banks' liquid asset holdings have been regressed against external sources of bank liquidity. See Reinhard Pohl, "Potentialorientierte Kreditpolitik in einer offenen Volkswirtschaft", *Konjunkturpolitik,* 4/1972, pp. 207 ff.

periods in the balancing item of the balance of payments, bank liquidity might only have been successfully restricted if effective controls had been extended to international payments connected with current account transactions.

iii) In both of the two phases of restraint during which the inflow problem became acute, the restrictive intent of the German monetary authorities was exercised against the background of sharply easing monetary conditions elsewhere, particularly in the United States. This obstacle might have been partly overcome in the first restrictive period by controlling interest-induced banking flows. In contrast, such selective measures were clearly insufficient in 1970, since institutional constraints on non-bank sector flows had been rapidly disappearing during the past few years.

More recently the authorities seem to have become increasingly aware of the consequences of growing financial integration for the conduct of domestic monetary policy and have allowed these tendencies to affect their policies in the field of international capital movements. Cash deposit regulations were introduced in March 1972 and tightened in June and December of the same year; the sale of domestic bonds to non-residents was subjected to licensing in June 1972 while the transfer of financial claims, other than securities to non-resirents against *quid pro quo,* was simultaneously made subject to obligatory registration with the central bank. The scope of direct controls on capital inflows was further enlarged in February and June 1973.

c) THE IMPACT OF MONETARY POLICY ON DOMESTIC FINANCIAL VARIABLES

The present section reviews, in qualitative terms, the apparent impact of monetary policy on changes in key intermediate financial variables —notably fluctuations in interest rates, bank credit, and the money supply— which are generally held to play a crucial role in the transmission of monetary policy effects to the real sector of the economy. The cyclical experience in non-bank financial markets is also commented upon, though the data available do not permit an analysis of developments in the short run. The discussion aims to assess, on the basis of a number of charts, the role of monetary policy or, more generally, the behaviour of financial institutions including the central bank, as determinants of changes in key financial variables. But short-run variations in most monetary variables should be conceived as the combined interaction of real and financial sectors (i.e. as partly endogenously determined), reflecting reactions of the economic system as a whole to current as well as past changes of monetary policy and to variations in exogenous influences not under the control of the central bank. Any visual interpretation given to causal relationships between time series that form part of a complex economic system inevitably involves subjective judgment. To guard, at least to some extent, against the obvious drawbacks of the approach adopted, the following analysis will take account of various complementary indicators related to the non-financial sector, as well as the rather limited econometric work available for Germany in which monetary policy variables and real variables have simultaneously been regressed against intermediate financial variables.

The developments of *domestic interest rates* have generally been consistent with the direction of bank liquidity management and changes in official lending rates (Charts 11 and 17). The response of interbank money market rates to changes in bank liquidity has been not only very quick but also quite large. Due to institutional arrangements (see page 35), shorter-term bank lending rates have moved closely parallel with the official discount rate. The Bundesbank has tended to keep official lending rates "in touch" with market rates and consistent with bank liquidity management. Occasional short-run deviations from this pattern have mainly occurred when official discount policy seemed to be hampered by balance of payments constraints. Prior to the liberalisation of bank lending rates in 1967, such deviations were probably reflected in banks' preferential (below maximum) lending rates which were granted to first-rate borrowers ("Sonderkonditionen"). Changes in actual lending rates may therefore have corresponded even more closely to movements in bank liquidity than suggested by the official ceiling rate shown in Chart 11. Deposit rates have quickly moved up against maximum or (since 1967) the banking associations' "recommended" interest rates which have been adjusted to changes in the discount rate, though generally with a lag. In addition, the tendency of the banks to react, until recently, in a quite regular manner to a reduction in their liquidity by initially reducing their purchase of bonds has produced an apparently quick response of bond rates to a change in bank liquidity. Changes in bond yields, in turn, have quickly been followed by long-term lending rates of mortgage banks.

In some other countries, the effects of initial monetary actions on bank reserves or liquidity spread from short-term interest rates to longer rates with somewhat longer time lags, at least partly reflecting the smaller share of the banking system in their financial markets. The apparently quick response of bond rates to changes in bank liquidity in Germany reflects the relative importance of the banks' role in the bond market, and the tendency of the banks to react to reductions of liquidity initially by reducing their purchase of bonds. When conditions become very stringent (as in 1960 and during part of 1966) they may actually reduce their holdings. Such behaviour by banks tended to stabilise the spread between short and long-term rates. This does not, of course, imply that observed interest rate developments can solely be attributed to changes in monetary policy and the behaviour of financial institutions. In restrictive periods, switches by non-bank borrowers from the longer to the shorter end of the market (see pages 17 and 69) also tended to raise short-term rates. But this move did not seriously affect the term structure of interest rates, at least in the first two restrictive periods, since security investment activity by the non-bank sectors followed the banks' portfolio behaviour and further pushed up longer rates. On the other hand, in 1970, despite a marked decline in banks' purchases of bonds, private households were attracted to the bond market through expectations that the rise in bond yields might only be short-lived. Thus the term structure of interest rates was reversed and short rates remained at levels higher than long rates until the end of the following year. Inflationary expectations are another important factor influencing the level of interest rates, notably at the longer end of the market, encouraging non-bank borrowers to accept higher interest costs and non-bank financial asset holders to demand higher yields. While such influences may not have been very marked up to the mid-1960's, their impact on the level of interest rates is likely to have been significant during the third restrictive policy period. Allowing for this factor, the impact of monetary policy on the level of interest rates was probably much stronger in the mid-1960's than suggested by visual observation of the levels of bank lending rates and bond yields.[11]

There is some evidence that the pace of *domestic bank credit* expansion during and following the three restrictive phases was related to changes in the stance of monetary policy (Charts 11 and 17). Indeed, credit expansion slowed down sharply in the course of 1960 and recovered strongly in 1961 closely in line with the development of the bank liquidity ratio, which the Bundesbank has been using as the main operating target and thus can be used as an indicator of the stance of monetary policy. During the second restrictive phase the slowdown was gradual during 1965 and 1966, although the liquidity ratio fell very markedly between early 1964 and mid-1966; but the pick-up in 1967 was strong. In the third phase, credit expansion slowed down considerably in the first half of 1969, but only moderately during the second half of 1969 and into 1970, differing somewhat from bank liquidity behaviour. A general impression is that the apparent response of bank credit to declining liquidity ratios is quite variable, as the somewhat different experiences in the three restrictive phases show. And the most recent evidence of the relationship is indicative of great instability; since mid-1970 a decline in the bank liquidity ratio to an unusually low level has been associated with a continued acceleration of bank credit.

If one looks more closely at the relationship over shorter periods, the impressions of instability are confirmed. In a number of instances, short-run variations in the growth rate of bank credit have, over periods of a few months, been nearly unrelated to changes in the bank liquidity ratio. One reason is the important role of capital flows; an inflow of non-bank funds increases bank liquidity and decreases the demand for credit. Thus, to the extent that the observed volume of bank credit is determined by demand, which may also be met from foreign sources, the normal positive association between changes in the bank liquidity ratio and credit is reversed. Instances of this occurred during the inflows in 1960 and even more clearly in 1971 when the substitution of domestic for foreign credit during the second half of the year exerted downward pressure on bank liquidity coinciding with an increase in the demand for bank credit.

The apparent instability of the relationship, which is confirmed by recent econometric work,[12] may be partly attributable also to the impact on

---

11. It should also be recalled that bank lending rates were subject to official ceilings in the earlier period and that monetary tightness may have been greater than indicated by movements in official maximum rates. In addition, new issues of bonds by the public sector and mortgage and communal banks were restricted by the government in 1965-66. Costs of long-term borrowing from outside the bond market appear to have shown, at least temporarily, a sharper rise than bond yields.

12. See Reinhard Pohl, ibid., p. 202. The author has related quarterly changes in total bank credit to variations in banks' free liquid assets, adopting various lag structures without significant results. In a recent more comprehensive study incorporating an independent variable representing non-bank credit demand, the contribution of changes in banks' free liquid asset holdings in explaining quarterly

bank lending behaviour resulting from changing credits risks (see page 44), to fluctuations in bank lending and deposit rates resulting from changes in interest race policy which were at times inconsistent with bank liquidity management (see page 53), and to non-bank financial behaviour (see page 71). But it would also seem to be closely linked to specific institutional arrangements and financial influences tending to produce movements in domestic short-term borrowing counter to the direction of credit policy and bank liquidity behaviour. One important reason for the latter phenomenon could be the fact that bank customers in Germany can generally draw in a quasi-automatic manner on previously arranged short-term credit lines and thus substitute short-term for longer-term bank credit if the latter becomes less freely available (see page 17). Since banks' short-term lending commitments, although of varying magnitude, were considerable at the beginning of each of the three restrictive periods, a quick and stable response of domestic credit expansion to a decline in bank liquidity may have been thwarted. Moreover, it is quite conceivable that official foreign exchange reserve policy has introduced an element of instability into observed relationships between changes in bank liquidity and short-term lending. The fact that non-resident deposits invested in short-term foreign assets have been exempted from reserve requirements has at times been a strong incentive to employ such deposits in foreign rather than domestic earning assets.

In contrast, a more regular impact of monetary policy on banks' longer-term lending activity and, in particular, savings and commercial banks' bond purchases is apparent and is confirmed by econometric work.[13] As bank liquidity contracted, banks tended to attach priority to satisfying the credit needs of communal and industrial borrowers consistent with existing institutional links (see page 19), while reducing their bond purchases. The reverse movement took place when bank liquidity increased. While these cyclical patterns in banks' bond purchases were rather stable during most of the period under review, the year 1971 saw a marked deviation from past experience: a strong rise in their bond purchases coincided with a decline in their liquidity ratio to a historically low level.

The fact that the German non-bank sectors could substitute domestic for foreign credits without difficulty implies that total domestic bank credit is not in itself a good indicator of German monetary conditions (i.e. credit availability) in the shorter run. The question is whether some other financial variables are more reliable indicators of general monetary conditions. One obvious such candidate is the *narrowly defined money supply* (M_1) which has generally been associated with the non-bank sectors' demand for transactions balances. There are some features of its development which

fluctuations in short-term bank credit was found to be low, while the coefficient derived for changes in banks' unutilised rediscount quotas was even negative. See Winand Kau, "Probleme der potentialorientierten Kreditpolitik", *Konjunkturpolitik*, 4/1972, pp. 226 ff. Both studies cover observation periods almost identical with the period here under review.

13. See Reinhard Pohl, *op. cit.*, and Winand Kau, *ibid.* The latter author has explicitly allowed for non-banks' supply of earning assets to banks as an additional explanatory variable. For further references see also OECD, *The Capital Market, International Capital Movements, Restrictions on Capital Operations in Germany*, Paris 1969, p. 33, and Deutsches Institut für Wirtschaftsforschung, "Wertpapiererwerb und Liquiditätspolitik der Sparkassen", *Wochenbericht*, 24/72, p. 215.

seem to suggest that the money supply did behave in an anti-cyclical way, notably the slowdown through 1959-60, and the pick-up through 1961; and the slowdown between late-1964 and mid-1966, and the subsequent reacceleration. Similarly, there was a continuous acceleration during most of 1970 and into early 1971. And a closer look at a number of other turning points shows developments not consistent with the timing of policy. Thus the slowdowns in 1959 and again in early 1964 seem to have begun too early to be explained as the effect of the policy restraints initiated during these two years; and the sharp deceleration at end-1962 had no obvious relation to monetary policy—which was, at this stage, more or less neutral.

The divergent developments in the narrow money supply and the bank liquidity ratio (the authorities' preferred operating target for most of the period under review) can to some extent be "explained" by balance of payments developments. A sudden movement of capital will affect both bank liquidity and private sector demand deposits, movements in which dominate fluctuations in the narrow money stock. However, the capital flow will cause sharper relative fluctuations in the volume of bank liquidity, which is the smaller of the two domestic monetary series, thus introducing considerable instability into the relationship between the bank liquidity ratio and the money supply. But there is evidence of another "explanation" of the volatility of the association between bank liquidity and the narrowly defined money supply in the short run. In all three boom periods there were occasions when accelerations or decelerations of demand deposits and time deposits were inversely related. This inverse relationship may be explained by, among other things, shifts in the relative growth rates of the demand and time deposits of the household and corporate sectors, or shifts in the non-bank sectors' propensity to hold time rather than demand deposits, reflecting changes in relative interest rates. This last mechanism was undoubtedly the predominant factor explaining the considerable shift from demand deposits into shorter-term time deposits in the mid-1960's, when official ceilings on bank deposits were gradually removed. Indeed, seasonal payments patterns in Germany suggest that time deposits at least up to three months' maturity could represent transactions balances, while time deposits up to four years' maturity, the bulk of which is held by the company sector and parts of the public sector (local authorities, social security system), can generally be assumed to constitute money substitutes that can, with relatively little cost or inconvenience, be converted into cash. The large-scale interest arbitrage operations between short and longer-term time deposits that occurred since the full liberalisation of bank deposit rates in 1967 would, in fact, indicate that it is both conceptually and practically difficult to establish a clear separation of transactions balances, likely to fall within the narrowly defined money supply, from the broad category of quasi-money time deposits.

These phenomena would suggest that it is more useful to look at the composite variable, the *broadly defined money supply* (M_2), as an indicator of general monetary conditions. This yields a series, the fluctuations of which correspond more closely than those of its components to the fluctuations of domestic credit expansion and the banking system's external assets taken together. Of course, in the most recent period, speculative flows and their reversal also played a role in the development of the banking system's net external assets, producing apparently erratic changes, particularly in time deposits and hence in M_2.

70

M_2 showed more or less the same pattern in the first half of the 1960's. However, the picture is different in the second half of the decade. M_2 ceased decelerating already during 1965, reaccelerated during 1966 and accelerated further in 1967. This development reflected the pronounced fluctuations of the balance of payments effects on domestic liquidity creation during this period (see page 56); the proceeds of increased foreign exchange inflows in 1966 were accumulated in the form of time deposits rather than M_1, reflecting a slowdown of economic activity and hence a weak demand for money balances for transaction purposes at least in some important domestic sectors. Such an episode clearly indicates the feedback of the real sector on the development of the financial sector, blurring the relationship between the bank liquidity ratio and broader monetary aggregates.

Among other exogenous financial influences not under the central bank's immediate control, the financial activity of the public sector had a distorting impact on the relationship between the bank liquidity ratio, on the one hand, and the money supply and bank credit, on the other. At times this influence may have been as important as that of capital flows (see pages 68 and 70). In 1967, for example, heavy reliance of the public sector on borrowing from domestic banks through the issuance of liquid debt (see page 55) increased the volume of bank liquidity. This would tend to induce a sharper rise in the bank liquidity ratio than in total credit and monetary expansion, even on the assumption that an increase in bank credit to the public sector and its increased cash disbursement did not affect bank credit to the private sector. On the other hand, the accumulation in 1970-71 of large public sector balances with the central bank tended to reduce the volume of bank liquidity and the money supply. Even if there was no increase in the private sector's bank borrowing to offset monetary contraction, the relationship between the liquidity ratio and the money stock should have been distorted by the different magnitudes of the bank liquidity and money series; and to the extent that there was an offsetting increase in bank lending to the private sector, a decline in bank liquidity was related to a more moderate reduction in the money supply and a *rise* in total bank credit (since the public sector did not use the accumulated balances for repaying its debt to the banking system).

To sum up the previous paragraphs, there is little evidence to suggest a stable impact of monetary policy on the main monetary aggregates, bank credit and the money stock (narrowly or broadly defined). The impact of bank liquidity management on bank credit has been influenced by, among other things, net inflows or outflows of capital and by the impact on M_1 from variations in relative interest rates. As regards the broad definition of the money supply (M_2), the survey of the main time series suggests that it was only during the first restrictive phase, i.e. in 1960, that the growth of M_2 was restrained by restrictive monetary policy. In 1966 —during what would *prima facie* be regarded as the clearest example of monetary restraint during the period under study—the growth rate rose as the year advanced.

As explained above, the authorities' influence on the availability of domestic bank credit through the control of bank liquidity has been weakened by disruptive capital flows between Germany and elsewhere. Moreover, in the case of Germany, the flow of loans by non-bank financial intermediaries (building and loan associations and insurance companies) has

71

tended to be procyclical—rising, albeit slightly, in periods of monetary tightness. In such periods, life insurance companies have reduced their purchases of bank debentures and increased their lending for housing purposes, often at preferential rates to their own policy holders, thus offsetting a decline in this type of lending by mortgage banks and savings banks. Even more important has been the temporary acceleration of building and loan associations' short-term "intermediate" credits at low interest rates, to be refinanced later through longer-term mortgage credits.

There seem to have been two major reasons why these financial intermediaries were able to expand their lending activity (notably to finance housebuilding) when that of the banking system was contracting. First, throughout the period under review a steady increase in the deposits of the building and loan associations (partly reflecting tax incentives to hold savings in this form) enabled them to build up substantial financial reserves invested mainly in bank deposits and loans to the banking system; these reserves amounted on average to as much as one quarter to one-third of their total assets and could easily be drawn upon to finance "intermediate" housing loans. Second, private savers placed a greater part of their savings with building and loan associations in periods of monetary restraint, partly in response to changes in tax incentives.

IV

THE IMPACT ON DEMAND AND ULTIMATE POLICY OBJECTIVES

In the present Part, an attempt is made to assess in a tentative way the impact of major policy changes and the ensuing adjustments of financial markets on private sector and local government expenditures in Germany. As a first step, turning points in the bank liquidity ratio (or major policy steps) and peaks or troughs in expenditure series possibly related to them will be reviewed. Since the liquidity ratio may not always be an appropriate measure of monetary "tightness" or "ease" (see pages 68, 69, 70 and 71), the evidence provided by developments in intermediate financial indicators (Part III [c]) is also examined. In this context, the likely transmission process of changes in financial conditions is tentatively discussed insofar as existing knowledge of spending behaviour and the structure of the economy permits such an evaluation. Influences other than those of monetary policy are discussed wherever they may have had a powerful effect in determining the observed behaviour of expenditures. This impressionistic analysis is supplemented by some econometric findings of the OECD Secretariat, based on a single-equation study. While the precise quantitative information about the impact of monetary policy on the real economy can be provided only by a comprehensive econometric model which estimates financial and real variables simultaneously, the evidence which has been obtained from the simple approach adopted seems useful in specifying the link between the monetary and real sectors.

a) INVENTORIES

Inventory investment, as well as entrepreneurs' judgment on existing stock levels in industry (Chart 19), reveals a strong cyclical pattern. Recorded peaks in stockbuilding rates and in optimistic sentiment of entrepreneurs with respect to inventory levels have followed the adoption of a restrictive stance of monetary policy with a relatively short lag (generally 2-4 quarters), while recoveries in stockbuilding have shown a somewhat irregular pattern in relation to changes in monetary policy. The pattern of interest rates seems to have been inversely related to the three cycles of stockbuilding observed during the period under review, the latter lagging somewhat behind the former. The first and third cycles also followed the turning points of monetary aggregates with some time lag, although the short-run instability of this type of expenditure makes it

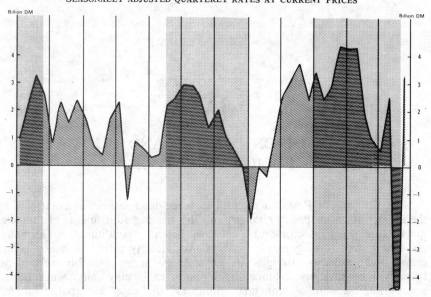

JUDGMENT ON LEVEL OF STOCKS

PERCENTAGE BALANCE OF REPLIES FROM ENTREPRENEURS

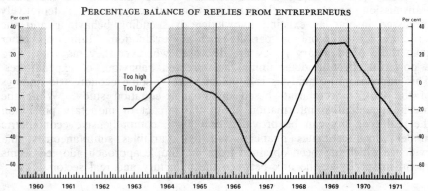

difficult to make an exact measurement of the length of the lags; on the other hand, the relationship between the two is not clear for the second inventory cycle.

Although the result of econometric work so far carried out in Germany[1] has not led to any firm conclusions as to the influence of financial conditions on stockbuilding, the regression analysis of the OECD Secre-

1. See Dietrich Lüdecke, *Ein ökonemetrisches Vierteljahresmodell für die Bundesrepublik Deutschland,* Tübingen 1969 ; Dirk van der Werf, *De westduitse economie in vijftien vergelijkingen,* Amsterdam 1971 ; Wilhelm Krelle, "Functioning of a Prognostication Model for the Western German Economy," *Economies et sociétés,* No. V/1971, pp. 1341-1391.

Chart 20. EQUATION FOR INVENTORY INVESTMENT
SEASONALLY ADJUSTED

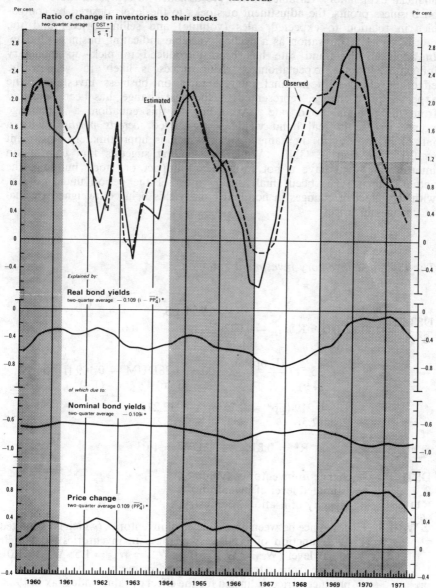

tariat supports the visual observations made in the preceding paragraph which point to a susceptibility of stock building to monetary influences, reflecting interest rate effects rather than availability effects. In the estimated equation which is shown below, the dependent variable is expressed as the percentage ratio of the quarterly change in inventories to the level of stocks

75

at the beginning of the quarter. The equation includes several non-financial explanatory variables which are assumed to represent the situation on business profits, the adjustment of stocks to the levels desired by companies in relation to expected sales (volume) and selling prices, and the rate of capacity utilisation as a cyclical variable indicating business climate. In addition, the bond rate has been introduced to pick up monetary influences.[2] Since expectation of rising prices is likely to weaken the effect of changes in nominal interest rates on business investment, the expected price change, represented by the past change, has been deducted from the nominal bond rate. According to this equation, a percentage point increase in real bond yields is associated, *ceteris paribus*, with a fall of inventories in the same quarter which is approximately equivalent to 0.15 per cent of GNP. While this finding suggests that changes in interest rates can have a not insignificant impact on stock building, the actual influence has been small during most of the period under review, with the effect of changes in nominal bond yields being outweighed by that of changes in prices.

The estimated inventory investment equation

$$\frac{DST^*}{S^*_{-1}} \times 100 = \underset{(2.6)}{0.069}\, KU_{-2} - \underset{(2.5)}{0.022}\, \frac{\overset{-5}{\underset{-1}{\Sigma}} W_t\, RES_t}{S^*_{-1}} \times 100$$

$$+ \underset{(4.9)}{35.517}\, \frac{(E/pp)^*}{S^*_{-1}} \times 100 + \underset{(3.6)}{1.38} DUM - \underset{(1.4)}{0.109}\, (i - \overline{pp}^0_4)^*$$

$$+ \underset{(2.5)}{0.219}\, (\overline{pp}^0_2 - 0.25\, \overline{pp}^0_8) - \underset{(5.2)}{12.275}$$

$$R^2 = 0.81 \qquad DW = 1.03$$

DST = change in inventories (volume).
S_{-1} = estimated level of inventories.
KU = capacity utilisation in industry.
$\overset{-5}{\underset{-1}{\Sigma}} W_t RES_t$ = difference between desired level of inventories (which is estimated as a function of GNP less changes in inventories) and their actual level ($W_{-1} = W_{-5} = 0.5$; $W_{-2} = W_{-3} = 1.5$; $W_{-4} = 1.0$).
E = income from entrepreneurship and property.
pp = producer prices adjusted for the effect of value-added tax in 1968.
$\overline{pp}^0_t$ = percentage change in producer prices over t quarters earlier.

2. Although bond issues are a minor source of companies' external funds, bond yields can be a good approximation for their average borrowing cost, since the term structure of interest rates is relatively stable in Germany (see page 18). Bank lending rates and deposit rates are only known as official ceiling rates prior to April 1967, and no time series is available on the cost of longer-term company borrowing in the form of straight bank loans or promissory notes (Schuldscheindarlehen).

i   = bond yield.
DUM   = dummy for inclement winter (1963 first quarter = 1.0).
*   = average of two quarters.
             (t-ratios in brackets; DW = Durbin-Watson).

Sources: Income, price and expenditure series and the rate of capacity utilisation are taken from quarterly data of Deutsches Institut für Wirtschaftsforschung (DIW) and seasonally adjusted by the OECD Secretariat. Quarterly figures for the level of inventories were estimated by the OECD Secretariat. Yields on bonds in circulation are published by the Deutsche Bundesbank.

b) BUSINESS FIXED INVESTMENT

Normally one would expect fixed investment expenditures to react somewhat more slowly than inventory accumulation to changes in monetary policy. There will typically be a lag between decisions to expand capacity and actual expenditures. Particularly if the backlog of unfinished projects is large or if suppliers are being constrained by capacity limitations, expenditures on fixed investment may continue rising for some time after plans for new projects begin to recede. For these reasons the following discussion of the possible effects of monetary policy on fixed investment will draw on actual expenditure data and on developments in orders for capital goods, as well as on indicators of business expectations. The expenditure data are shown in Chart 21, and those relating to orders in Chart 22, together with the results of business opinion surveys reporting views on the current and expected situation. Table 11 summarises observed lags from the adoption of restrictive monetary policy stance to cyclical weakening of the main expenditure series. The observed lags were notably long in the third restrictive period, when short-lived tax measures distorted the quarterly expenditure figures reported by companies.

The turning-point analysis does not, in itself, prove the existence of a causal timing relationship. What follows is an impressionistic interpretation of the role of monetary and other influences on this type of expenditure. It is based on a general review of how financial and non-financial factors which may affect the course of business investment activity developed, notably in the three phases of restraint and in one reflationary phase.

i) During the first restrictive period, the contribution of monetary policy to a deceleration of the private fixed investment boom may not have been of crucial importance. Growth of monetary aggregates and the development of interest rates point to a marked relaxation of credit restraint two quarters before the peak in manufacturing and non-manufacturing investment and about one quarter prior to the decline in domestic orders for capital goods. While this does not exclude the possibility of a lagged effect of changes in interest rates on business fixed investment, it seems difficult to prove the existence of "availability" effects which are likely to work relatively quickly. On the other hand, the weakening of private investment coincided with

77

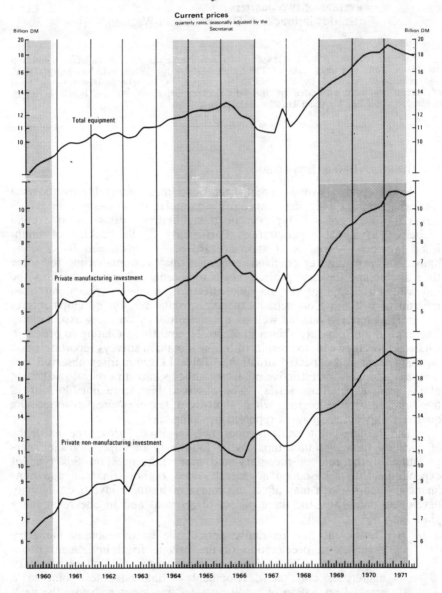

a squeeze on company profits and internal funds, heavy exchange market speculation and revaluation of the deutschemark in March 1961. Revaluation and the ensuing accelerating decline in foreign orders could have depressed sales expectations, particularly in manufacturing, since the future development of foreign demand and the volume impact of the DM revaluation may have

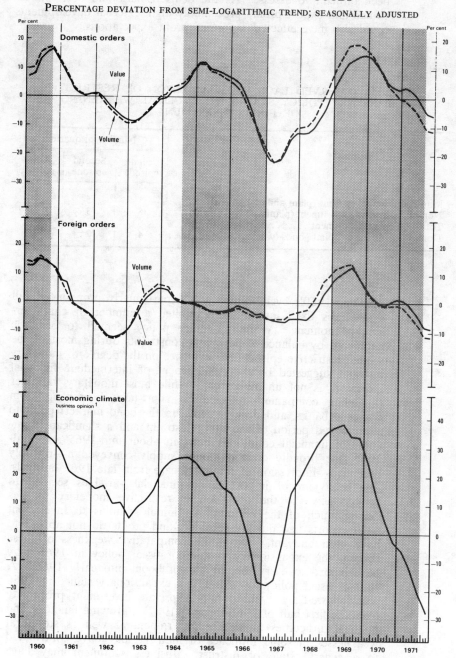

Chart 22. ORDERS FOR CAPITAL GOODS

PERCENTAGE DEVIATION FROM SEMI-LOGARITHMIC TREND; SEASONALLY ADJUSTED

1. Difference between optimistic and pessimistic replies of entrepreneurs to the survey about judgment on the current business situation and expectations for coming six months.

been difficult to assess. As the deutschemark had been undervalued and export profits presumably high, external developments could also have affected exporters' profit expectations.

TABLE 11. OBSERVED LAGS FROM ADOPTION OF RESTRICTIVE
MONETARY POLICY STANCE TO CYCLICAL WEAKENING
OF FIXED INVESTMENT

	Number of quarters		
	First episode	Second episode	Third episode
Manufacturing investment (plant and equipment)	5	5	8
Non-manufacturing investment (plant and equipment)....	5	3	7
Total equipment investment	6	6	7
Domestic orders for capital goods (values)	4	2	2

ii) The mid-1960's cycle, which saw a particularly pronounced fall in business fixed investment, exhibited a number of characteristic phenomena. While monetary policy seemed to be little hampered by balance-of-payments constraints during most of the second restrictive episode, the evidence on the degree of monetary restraint suggested by the development of intermediate financial indicators is not unambiguous. While most monetary variables (including companies' reliance on short-term borrowing from domestic banks, and developments on the bond market) point to a prolonged period of monetary restraint and a significant tightening of financial conditions between about mid-1965 and mid-1966, the broadly defined money supply conveyed a—possibly deceptive—impression of monetary ease from late 1965 onwards. The behaviour of important non-financial variables seemed to be conducive to the operation of restrictive monetary policies during much of the period. An initial stimulus to investment from exports had quickly subsided, and profits do not appear to have been buoyant. Given the comparative weakness of these stimuli, the expansionary posture of fiscal policy in 1965 may have helped to carry the investment boom into early 1966. A shift of fiscal policy towards a less expansionary stance in 1966 was followed by a sharp fall in private investment propensity from the first half of 1966 through 1967. Growing financial and political difficulties facing the government as well as structural weaknesses in some branches of industry may have contributed to a general state of distrust. Business sentiment may have been somewhat aggravated by a further rise in the official discount rate in May 1966 which appears to have engendered powerful announcement effects rather than conspicuous changes in financial markets.

80

iii) The task of reconstituting confidence in 1967-68 was not an easy one. Temporary tax incentives were quickly taken up by investors, but demand and output in investment goods industries fell sharply after the measures had expired. And a vigorous joint effort by the central bank and by the Federal and Länder governments in managing the public debt (see page 55) was required to satisfy banks' demand for liquid assets and to bring down domestic interest rates to levels conducive to long-term borrowing and consolidation of companies' short-term debt. Business fixed investment began to pick up in early 1968.

iv) During the third restrictive period, the coincidence of major developments in domestic investment series on the one hand, and exchange rate developments and changes in foreign orders on the other, is again apparent. Most financial indicators suggest a rapid increase in monetary restraint during the six months following the DM revaluation in October 1969, a development conspicuously different from the earlier revaluation experience. It is conceivable that restrictive monetary measures temporarily reinforced the dampening effect of revaluation on domestic investment demand and business expectations. However, from about mid-1970 onwards, capital inflows placed severe limits on the control of interest rates and monetary aggregates by the central bank, and the termination of the investment boom in 1971 may mainly be attributable to the floating of the deutschemark and the squeeze, since 1970, on companies' profit and self-financing margins.

There is some econometric evidence in Germany that changes in interest rates are most consistently related to fluctuations in business fixed investment.[3] The OECD Secretariat has also undertaken regression analysis to test this relationship. The adopted investment function, which is shown below, has been fitted to the period from the third quarter of 1960 to the second quarter of 1972. It incorporates as the dependent variable the quarterly level of business fixed investment as a per cent of actual capital stock. An explanatory variable related to profitability has been introduced in the form of the real rate of return on capital which is represented as the ratio of income from entrepreneurship and property (deflated by an investment goods price index) to capital stock. The accelerator hypothesis has been adopted in its original form assuming that the *level* of investment is influenced by *changes* in output. Since the influence on investment resulting from profit and output developments is likely to be modified by actual levels of capacity utilisation, utilisation rates in industry have also been introduced. In addition the bond yield[4] has been introduced as a variable representing monetary influences. As in the equation for stockbuilding, expectations of rising prices are assumed to weaken the restrictive impact of the rise in nominal interest rates.

The coefficient for the interest rate variable has the expected negative sign and points to a potentially rather powerful influence of interest rates;

3. Joachim Rosette ("Oekonometrische Investitionsfunktionen für Konjunktur-modelle", *Konjunkturpolitik*, 3/1971, pp. 139-219) found that market interest rates had a significant explanatory value in a broad spectrum of investment functions in German industry.

4. See footnote to page 76.

the estimated equation indicates that a percentage rise in (nominal) bond yields is related with a lag of two quarters to a drop of fixed investment, whose magnitude in money terms varies according to the scale of the economy in that quarter (for the first quarter of 1971, about DM 0.75 billion at 1963 prices) and is equivalent to about 0.6 per cent of real GNP. However, the actual role of interest rates has been small during most of the observation period. Chart 23, where the contribution of the composite real interest rate variable is broken down by its two components, reveals that this is largely attributable to divergent developments of nominal interest rates and prices. Moreover, since the second half of the 1960's real interest rates have tended to develop in a destabilising manner—rising during the 1966-68 period of under-utilisation of resources and low levels of business fixed investment, and falling quite markedly during the excessive 1969-71 investment boom.

The estimated business fixed investment equation

$$\frac{I}{K_{-1}} \times 100 = - \underset{(8.1)}{0.0368} \ (i - 0.66 \ \overline{PY^0_6})_{-2} + \underset{(6.4)}{0.0116} \ (KU_{-1} + KU_{-2})$$

$$+ \underset{(0.6)}{0.0032} \ \frac{E/PI}{K_{-2}} - \underset{(3.6)}{0.129} DUM + \underset{(4.7)}{0.0124} \ \overline{Y^0_4} - \underset{(3.1)}{0.908}$$

$$R^2 = 0.87 \qquad\qquad DW = 1.58$$

I	= business fixed investment (quarterly volume figure).
K	= capital stock.
i	= bond yield.
PY^0_6	= GNP price deflator (percentage change over 6 quarters earlier).
KU	= capacity utilisation in industry.
E	= income from entrepreneurship and property.
PI	= price deflator for business fixed investment.
DUM	= dummy for inclement winter (1963 first quarter = 1.0).
Y^0_4	= real GNP (percentage change over 4 quarters earlier).
	(t-ratios in brackets; DW = Durbin-Watson).

Source: Income, price and expenditure series and the rates of capacity utilisation are taken from quarterly data of Deutsches Institut für Wirtschaftsforchung (DIW) and seasonally adjusted by the OECD Secretariat. Quarterly figures for capital stock were obtained by simple interpolation from official annual estimates. Bond yields are published by the Deutsche Bundesbank.

The above econometric evidence is consistent with the view that given the relatively short economic life time of machinery and equipment in modern industry, the effect of a small change in interest rates may often be outweighed by risks and uncertainties attaching to future sales, selling prices, replacement costs, etc. German enterprises, notably bigger companies, are also known largely to eliminate short-run fluctuations in market interest rates from internal calculations by applying rather stable standard

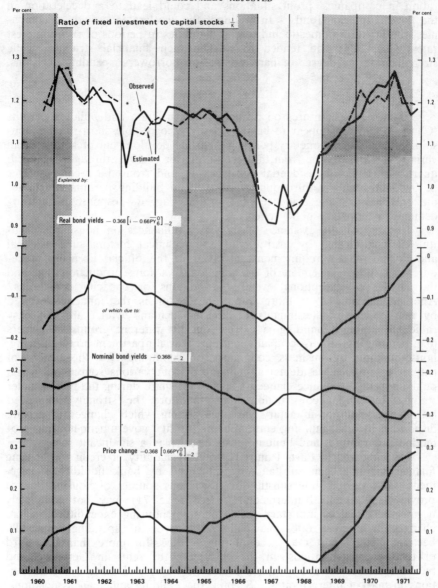

Chart 23. EQUATION FOR BUSINESS FIXED INVESTMENT
SEASONALLY ADJUSTED

Per cent

Ratio of fixed investment to capital stocks $\frac{I}{K}$

1.3

Observed

1.2

*

1.1

Estimated

1.0

Explained by:

0.9

Real bond yields $-0.368\left[i-0.66\overline{PY}\frac{0}{6}\right]_{-2}$

0

of which due to:

−0.1

Nominal bond yields $-0.368i_{-2}$

−0.2

−0.2

−0.3

Price change $-0.368\left[0.66\overline{PY}\frac{0}{6}\right]_{-2}$

0.3

0.2

0.1

0

1960 1961 1962 1963 1964 1965 1966 1967 1968 1969 1970 1971

Sources: Deutscher Institut für Wirtschaftsforschung, Deutsche Bundesbank, OECD.
* Break due to the severe winter 1962/63.

rates ("kalkulatorische Zinsen"). Nevertheless, substantial increases in interest rates may influence investment decisions. Moreover, German enterprises' use of own capital appears to be relatively low on an international comparison, while they carry a considerable volume of short-term debt

83

at flexible interest rates which are often linked to the official discount rate; a rise in interest rates could therefore imply a significant deterioration in companies' profit situations and could lead to a deceleration in the flow of internal funds. In addition, the accelerated growth of companies' shorter-term domestic and foreign liabilities in periods of rising interest rates (Chart 24) had tended to weaken their financial structure while strengthening the degree of bank control on borrowers' spending decisions.

c) HOUSING

Data on expenditures on residential construction and building permits (Chart 25) do not appear to bear an easily recognisable short-run relationship to changes in monetary policy, nor to the development of key financial variables. The decline from the second quarter of 1966 through the fourth quarter of 1967 in residential construction, and from the second quarter of 1966 through the third quarter of 1967 in building permits constitutes the only *prima facie* evidence of a—rather lagged—response of housing demand to monetary policy effects.

Testing for the existence of monetary influences on housing expenditure is complicated by institutional and technical factors such as legal and documentation requirements involved in the official licensing procedure and the arrangement of housing loans, a long production lag, and the impact of exceptional weather conditions or capacity constraints.[5] Another, possibly even more important, factor is the influence exerted by non-monetary determinants of housing demand which are not easy to identify. Housebuilding is carried out by different groups of owners (e.g. building by owner-occupants, entrepreneurial apartment-house building, house-building by business companies or communes for the benefit of employees or local residents) and financed from various sources of which public housing assistance claimed a significant share during the period under study. Residential construction may, therefore, be strongly influenced by a variety of non-monetary variables among which changes in private disposable income, building entrepreneurs' profits, government housing promotion programmes and building costs could play a significant role.

As indicated in Parts I and III, total availability of credit for housing finance has not been substantially influenced by bank liquidity management. But the possible substitution of various sources of housing finance provided by financial intermediaries (see page 71) may not completely negate the effect of monetary policy on total housing expenditure. First, changes in interest rates may affect this type of spending, especially because interest cost may account, on average, for more than one third of total construction cost in the calculation of rents in Germany, and public subsidies do not completely insulate housing demand from fluctuations in market interest rates. Second, the building and loan associations, which have typically been able to step up their lending activity in restrictive periods, supply the bulk of second mortgage loans, mainly to owner-occupants and little to other types of owners, and their "intermediate" credits are no lasting substitute for long-term first mortgage loans. Some groups of borrowers show a preference for long-term, fixed interest mort-

---

5. Detailed financial data suggest, for example, a fairly regular average lag of about three quarters from the arrangement of housing loans to actual credit flows.

Chart 24. COMPANIES' SHORT-TERM DEBT

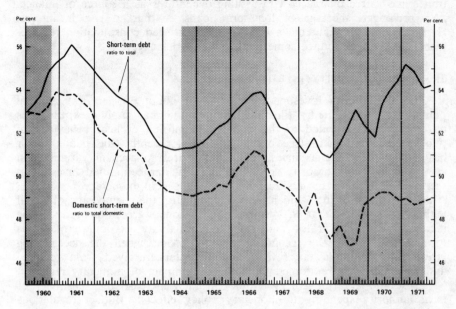

Chart 25. HOUSING ACTIVITY

PERCENTAGE DEVIATION FROM SEMI-LOGARITHMIC TREND; SEASONALLY ADJUSTED

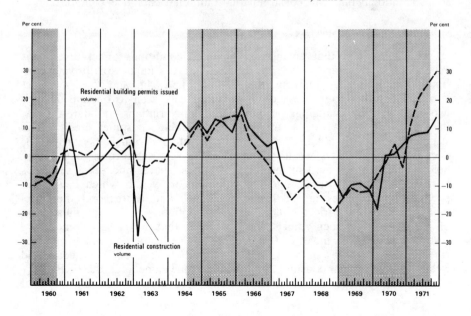

85

gage loans which only the mortgage banks can supply in sufficient quantitities and at reasonable cost by issuing debentures as a source of finance. Any prolonged shortage of long-term loans or marked rise in interest rates may, therefore, create a backlog of unsatisfied consolidation requirements that could produce some dampening of demand.

d) LOCAL AUTHORITY INVESTMENT

Local authority investment accounts for about 60 per cent of total public fixed investment. Fluctuations in communal capital expenditures have greatly contributed to the rather destabilising cyclical behaviour of public fixed investment (see page 13). Until recently, the public sector has tended to adjust its investment expenditures to cyclical variations in tax revenue; local authority spending, in particular communal investment, seems also to have been susceptible to changes in monetary conditions. Although the existing evidence is incomplete, the behaviour of local authorities suggests that their spending decisions were influenced by the increase in interest rates and reduced availability of long-term funds towards the end of the second restrictive episode, when the decelerating growth of communal tax revenue and transfers received from regional authorities strongly reinforced the restrictive impact of monetary restraint.

Institutional arrangements would, in fact, increase the sensitivity of local authority spending to monetary policy effects. Budget regulations and the manner in which supervisory powers are exercised by the regional authorities limit the extent to which debt servicing may absorb current revenue. As many local authorities, especially larger cities, have operated their budgets close to stipulated debt limits, any marked increase in interest rates may have affected their spending decisions. Moreover, there are restrictions on communal short-term borrowing and on the flexible utilisation of accumulated financial reserves for the financing of investment. Prolonged shortages in the supply of long-term funds could, therefore, act as an additional financial constraint on communal capital expenditure.

e) PRIVATE CONSUMPTION

To the extent that changes in financial conditions affect investment expenditures, monetary policy has had an indirect impact on private consumption. It seems unlikely that it has had, in addition, a direct impact. In other countries such direct effects are seen to operate through two channels: by changing, primarily through variations in interest rates, the wealth of the private sector, and by rationing consumer credit. The structure of wealth holdings by German private individuals (see page 18) does not suggest that a wealth effect could be very significant: total household financial assets held in the form of bonds, shares and other securities have been relatively small, and the variations in wealth which have been produced by changes in the return on bonds and shares are, therefore, modest compared with the flow of consumption. If, as an illustration of the scope for such effects, one assumes that a phase of monetary restraint were to produce a 10 per cent fall in the market value of securities in the portfolios of households, and that the coefficient of household wealth in the German consumption function is the same as in the FRB-MIT-Penn model of the United States economy (a little above 0.5), annual consumption expenditures might at most be reduced by less than DM 0.5 billion.[6] This should be seen against the fact that annual private consumption was around DM 400 billion in 1970-71.

Consumer instalment debt plays a rather unimportant though growing role in Germany. In 1969, for example, the increase in all household sector debt, excluding mortgages and other housing loans, was only around 1 per cent of total consumption expenditure. No attempt has been made to control the terms of consumer instalment credit for purposes of demand management, by creating official regulations pertaining to maximum repayment periods or minimum down payments.

f) AGGREGATE DEMAND, BALANCE OF PAYMENTS AND PRICES

The above analysis of the behaviour of various demand components suggests that, generally, the impact of monetary policy changes on *total domestic demand* has depended mainly on the effect on business investment. Indeed the turning points of total internal demand were largely influenced by those of business investment in stocks and fixed non-residential capital formation (Chart 27). During the first episode of monetary restraint, the slowdown of total internal demand took place concomitantly with the deceleration of non-residential fixed investment—about five quarters after the introduction of restrictive monetary policy and two quarters

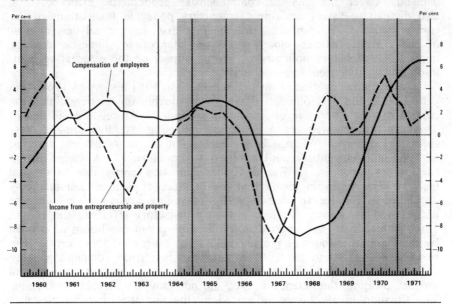

Chart 26. CYCLICAL DEVELOPMENT OF WAGES AND PROFITS

SMOOTHED PERCENTAGE DEVIATION FROM SEMI-LOGARITHMIC TREND; SEASONALLY ADJUSTED

6. The value of the securities portfolio was approximately DM 70 billion at end-1970; a 10 per cent change—a very significant one—is therefore DM 7 billion, which multiplied by the coefficient of household wealth (a little more than 0.05) gives an effect of less than DM 0.5 billion over a period of 3-4 quarters.

after the onset of weakening of stock building. During the second and third periods of restrictive monetary policy, aggregate domestic demand began to decelerate about one quarter after the start of the slowdown in inventory investment (which in turn followed the introduction of restrictive monetary policy with lags of two and four quarters respectively) and two to three quarters earlier than the downturn of non-residential fixed investment. The difference in the lag relationship between stockbuilding and total internal demand (which was shorter in the latter two periods of restraint than in the first episode) was largely due to the fact that the downswing in private inventory investment in the latter two periods was sharper than in the first period of monetary restraint. While the exact timing of recovery of total internal demand in the first period of ease is not clear, it was approximately similar to the timing of the pick-up in stockbuilding and fixed non-residential investment (about two quarters after the relaxation of monetary policy) in the second phase when fiscal policy was expansionary against the background of monetary ease. Changes in private consumption also tended to magnify fluctuations of total internal demand in a direction consistent with the changes in the stance of monetary policy. But it is, as already indicated, difficult to quantify the direct effect of monetary policy on private consumption. Throughout the period under review, fluctuations in residential construction and public current expenditure were relatively small and had no important direct impact on the course of aggregate domestic demand.

The tentative nature of the assessment of the effect of monetary policy on various types of expenditure hardly permits a quantitative evaluation of the contribution of monetary policy to changes in aggregate domestic demand. Given the lack of comprehensive econometric evidence, it is also difficult to assess the role of monetary policy in fluctuations of the *current balance of payments*. But the fact that the cyclical development of the current balance closely reflected changes in domestic demand implies that monetary policy had a strong impact on the external account, insofar as it influenced domestic activity.

After the revaluation of the deutschemark in 1961 and up to 1964—the period when the development of GNP was roughly on its trend line—the current balance was more or less in equilibrium or showed a small deficit. The year 1965 showed a sizeable deficit, reflecting excessive demand pressures in Germany. When a better balance of the economy was restored in 1966, the current account reverted to equilibrium. A large current surplus developed in 1967 and 1968. This was partly due to cyclical factors. The recession meant that the pressure of demand fell markedly in Germany relative to that typically prevailing abroad. This element disappeared as activity regained a more satisfactory level; by the end of 1968 the economy was approaching full employment conditions as defined by the German authorities (an unemployment ratio of 0.8 per cent). But in marked contrast to the 1965 experience when strong demand pressure at home was accompanied by a swing of Germany's current account into a deficit position, the balance in 1969 did not show a noticeable weakening. The situation in 1969 was influenced by the fact that demand pressures were strong in many other countries also. Nevertheless, there are indications that pressures were relatively stronger in Germany than elsewhere. The persistence of a large current account surplus in these conditions

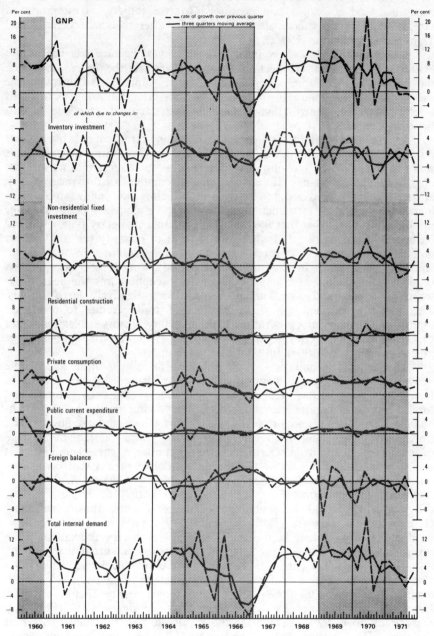

Chart 27. GROWTH OF INTERNAL DEMAND
SEASONALLY ADJUSTED ANNUAL RATE; CONSTANT PRICES

provided a measure of the fundamental disequilibrium that had developed. Not much of the effect of the 1969 deutschemark revaluation came through in 1970. Exports in that year reflected, to a large degree,

89

orders booked before the revaluation; furthermore, the price elasticity of foreign demand for an important portion of German goods seems to have been low, and prices abroad continued to rise rapidly. Restoration of external equilibrium was finally achieved only after the deutschemark had again been revalued in 1971.

The impact of monetary policy on the *capital balance* has been more evident. While Part III Section *(b)* has examined the extent to which the inflow of speculative and interest-sensitive capital has frustrated the use of monetary policy in restrictive periods, the following paragraphs briefly review the contribution of German monetary policy to capital outflows as well as to inflows.

In the first period of restraint, while long-term capital movements remained negligible, there was a large inflow of short-term capital. This was partly due to the growing discrepancy between interest rate movements at home and abroad. Moreover, the speculative disturbances which appear to have placed a dominant role in inducing such inflows took place immediately after the introduction of the restrictive monetary policy package in mid-1960, suggesting that the adoption of tighter monetary policy sparked off speculative activity. It is therefore difficult to quantify the total (direct and indirect) effect of monetary policy on capital inflows in that period with any precision. In the subsequent period of monetary ease, inflows of short-term capital were small. The main exception was the year 1962, when the errors and omissions item recorded a relatively large surplus. This possibly reflected the rising receipts of trade credits following an upturn of German imports, rather than monetary factors. Net long-term capital movements were also small, except in 1963 which saw an upsurge in non-residents' portfolio investments in Germany.

During the second period of restraint, there was little speculative activity in the foreign exchange market, as evidenced by the pattern of forward exchange rates (Chart 18). The inflow of banking funds and foreign portfolio capital remained negligible, owing partly to the Withholding Tax Scheme and protective measures against banking flows. The simultaneous tightening of monetary conditions abroad at the initial stage of monetary restraint in Germany also discouraged capital inflows. It was only in the latter part of the second restrictive period that companies reacted to the gradual tightening of monetary conditions at home by increasing foreign borrowing. In the second period of monetary ease, the long-term capital accounts showed large deficits, mostly reflecting German capital exports. Both non-monetary capital and banking flows produced a large deficit in the initial stage of monetary relaxation. The reversal of these flows in 1968 largely reflected new speculative activity.

During the third period of restraint, not only speculative activity but also changes in relative monetary conditions at home and abroad exerted an influence on capital flows. Expectations of a parity change attracted large amounts of funds in the second and third quarters of 1969, and massive outflows took place after the revaluation in the final quarter of the year. The inflows in 1970 and early 1971, however, were influenced by the fact that continuous monetary stringency in Germany and the decline of Euro-currency rates had turned interest differentials clearly in favour of Germany (Chart 18). The inflows were basically short-term and took place both through and outside the banking system. Capital inflows in the spring of 1971 were again partly the result of higher interest rates in Germany which kept uncovered interest differentials in favour of Germany. . Moreover, speculative activity tended to weaken the forward dollar and provided a strong incentive to "normal" capital inflows on a covered basis; it also lowered interest rates on the Euro-DM market and induced German companies to borrow in that market. Large outflows followed the floating of the Deutschemark in early May, and there was little movement during the subsequent months when monetary policy was relaxed.

External developments also complicated the German authorities' task of achieving the *main internal policy objective:* to contain price increases within reasonable bounds under the tighter labour supply conditions. In the early 1960's and in the latter stage of the most recent cycle, price increases reached new peak levels (Chart 1), similar only to those experienced during the Korean boom in 1951. The most important reason for these developments was inflationary pressures abroad from which the German economy could not be sufficiently protected despite the 1961 and 1969 revaluations. In the case of Germany, where both imports and exports occupy high shares of GNP, domestic prices were not only recurrently affected by export-induced boom conditions, but also through the direct links between foreign and domestic prices.

This does not imply, however, that German monetary policy was unable to play any role in the achievement of price stability during the period under review. The OECD Secretariat's econometric findings suggest that a measure of domestic demand pressure is a significant explanatory variable both for the German wage and price equations.[7] There is little evidence that the response of prices and wages to changes in demand pressures has weakened since the mid-1960's when the price development was favourable, due largely to relatively low rates of capacity utilisation. It may be that the tendency of companies to administer retail prices has been stronger in recent years: the increase since the mid-1960's in company mergers could have discouraged price competition; moreover, trade unions have been more agressive at wage negotiation tables during the most recent boom. But the bargaining policies of trade unions seem to have responded rather flexibly to the effect on export-oriented industries of a floating deutschemark. The rapid increase in prices during the most recent years can probably still be interpreted, at least partly, as a result of the acceleration of inflationary trends abroad and excess demand at home. The effects of restrictive monetary policy have been weakened by disruptive capital flows, and the 1969 revaluation came too late to shield the economy against international price developments. Lagged upward adjustments in public sector and agricultural prices have also tended to preserve inflationary pressures over an unusually long period.

---

7. OECD: *Inflation, the Present Problem,* Report by the Secretary-General, December 1970.

V

SUMMARY AND CONCLUDING REMARKS

This paper has described the uses of German monetary policy from the latter months of 1959 to the end of 1971. During that period there were three phases of economic expansion and excess demand—typically generated by an upturn in exports followed by an investment boom—and one recession. In the early stages of recovery from the recession, monetary policy worked closely together with fiscal policy to ensure the financing of counter-cyclical budgets and to overcome the financial constraints felt by some Länder and local authorities. In 1967, fiscal policy played a major role in the recovery from recession. Moreover, measures were introduced in the 1967 Law for Stability and Growth to permit a more flexible use of tax policies and to strengthen the central authorities' control over public authority borrowing and expenditures. Some of these measures were used during the recent inflationary phase. But the main burden of demand restraint was borne by monetary policy, particularly in the first two restrictive episodes.

During the period under review, there were several important factors which ought to have provided a favourable background to active use of monetary policy in Germany:

i) The large share of bank borrowing in the external finance of the business sector and public authorities and existing institutional links should have facilitated a smooth and quick transmission of the authorities' actions on the banking system to the non-bank sectors.

ii) The substitutability of various sources of housing finance provided by financial intermediaries had tended to insulate the housing market from the effect of restraint on bank credit. While this may have reduced the impact of monetary policy on real demand, it also enabled the authorities to pursue restrictive monetary policy more vigorously than would otherwise have been the case, since they could be less concerned about the adverse impact on a sector to which a high social priority is given.

iii) The predominance of banks in the capital market tended to produce a quicker and greater impact of monetary policy on long-term rates than in countries where the banks are specialised in short-term finance.

iv) The authorities' scope for increasing pressure on financial markets was little hampered by short-run problems of debt management.

Compared with some other countries, the volume of marketable public authority debt outstanding, in relation to gross national product, is rather small; the proportion in short-term debt is very small.

It has been against this background that the German authorities have sought to influence domestic financial conditions through control over the volume of bank liquidity and the liquidity ratio. The main quantitative instruments employed have been changes in minimum reserve ratios and reductions in rediscount quotas. Changes in the interest rates charged by the Bundesbank on its lending to banks complemented its quantitative measures. On the other hand, the central bank has not, until recently, attempted to ration its credit to control the supply of reserve money. Although the banks have not been allowed to have automatic right to borrow from the Bundesbank against collateral, sizeable unused margins have been left within rediscount quotas for the banking system as a whole, and its access to central bank credit has been automatic at the prevailing discount rate. Neither does the Bundesbank appear to have sought directly to influence the pace of individual banks' loan expansion in the course of its business dealing with them.

Bank liquidity management and changes in official lending rates have generally been followed, with a relatively short time lag, by parallel changes in non-bank sectors' costs of borrowing from domestic financial institutions and through raising funds in the capital market, at least partly due to the dominant role of the banking system in financial markets. Cyclical changes in the debt structure of the non-bank sectors were also fairly regular; interest-induced shifts in non-banks' borrowing preferences and the impact of liquidity management on banks' lending policies tended to raise the share of shorter-term liabilities in total credit flows from financial intermediaries to the non-bank sectors in periods of monetary restraint.

On the other hand, the response of domestic bank credit and the money supply has been somewhat unstable. They usually moved in a direction consistent with the stance of policy, but with a considerable time-lag; on occasions, however, they moved in the wrong direction. This irregular pattern seems to have been at least partly due to the long and short-run changes in the banks' portfolio selection which destabilise the relationship between bank liquidity and interest-earning assets. The non-monetary sectors' behaviour, including unpredictable changes in the use of unutilised overdraft facilities accumulated in preceding periods of monetary ease, has also been an additional element of instability. But, more than anything else, the authorities' effort to change the course of monetary aggregates in the desired direction was partially negated by the balance of payments, notably by capital flows. In restrictive periods, inflows of banking funds and non-monetary capital complicated the authorities' task of putting pressure on bank liquidity to decelerate credit and monetary expansion. Moreover, even when the authorities were able to offset the undesirable impacts of the foreign exchange inflow on bank liquidity, the direct monetary impact of non-monetary capital transactions weakened their influence over the monetary aggregates.

Thus, in addition to policy actions to offset the undesirable domestic monetary impact of capital flows, the authorities also tried to limit capital flows themselves through various controls. These measures were, however,

94

of only limited success. One of the major limitations was the substitutability of different types of capital inflows, particularly in periods of heavy
speculation. Indeed, strong revaluation expectations in 1960-61 and 1969
appear to have undermined the authorities' protective measures, as speculative pressures were diverted from banking funds to non-bank capital
following the introduction of tighter controls on the flow of banking funds.
In 1960, tight monetary policy was abandoned at the height of the boom,
as it seemed to have accelerated unwanted capital inflows offsetting the
initial restrictive effect of monetary policy. In 1970 and early 1971 capital
inflows also tended to nullify the authorities' efforts. In a sense, the
difficulty of managing domestic monetary conditions during most of the
1960's was implicit in the behaviour of the German economy. The infre-
quent need for Germany to be concerned with problems of underemployed
resources and the priority given to containing inflation no doubt played
a role in strengthening the competitive position of the deutschemark and
prepared the ground for speculative capital inflows. It should be noted,
however, that although the large and irregular capital flows were to a
considerable extent speculative, differences in monetary conditions between
Germany and other financial markets were also a major factor at times.

The extent of the restrictive impact of German monetary policy on
the real economy seems to have depended mainly on its effects on the
course of business investment. Generally, the contribution of changes in
inventories to fluctuations in total internal demand was larger than that of
non-residential fixed capital formation. On average, the deceleration of
stock building occurred about two to four quarters after the Bundesbank
began to apply restrictive policies, while a levelling-out in the course of
the business sector's fixed capital expenditures followed the adoption of
restrictive monetary policy with a relatively long lag (generally five to
six quarters). Changes in business confidence and in plans to invest
occurred sooner. The extent and the speed of these changes varied, depending on the underlying strength of current demand in relation to supply
possibilities (including supply conditions in foreign countries) and other
non-monetary influences on business expectations. For the important
manufacturing sector, changes in foreign demand for German exports
seem to have been of significant importance. The apparent strong effects
on demand of the 1966 tightening of monetary policy seem attributable
partly to the relative weakness of foreign order inflows during most of
the mid-1960's upswing and partly to the procyclical behaviour of public
investment, aggravating recessionary developments in 1966-67. The psy-
chological background was accordingly more favourable to monetary
restraint than was the case in 1969-70 when the external environment
made it very difficult to take effective measures of restraint.

In the transmission of German monetary policy to the real economy,
changes in interest rates seem to have been more important than credit
availability effects. Indeed, the OECD Secretariat's econometric findings
suggest that, *ceteris paribus,* a percentage point increase in real bond
yields (an approximation for companies' average borrowing cost) is
related to a fall in corporate inventories in the same quarter equivalent
to about 0.15 per cent of GNP and a decline, with an average lag of two
quarters, in private fixed non-residential investment amounting to about
0.6 per cent of GNP. While this evidence indicates that monetary policy

can have an important influence on business investment through changing interest rates, policy contribution to the stabilisation of this demand component seems to have been small in most of the period under review, even on the assumption that observed changes in nominal interest rates have been due entirely to monetary policy changes. In fact the impact of actual changes in nominal rates has often been outweighed by that of price changes.

Among other types of private demand, the housing sector seems to have been relatively insensitive to short-run changes in monetary conditions, although a prolonged rise in long-term interest rates and a marked deceleration in first-mortgage lending by the banking system might have exerted a restrictive impact on demand for new construction. Private consumption also seems to have been little affected by the immediate thrust of credit policy. Consumer instalment debt is relatively unimportant, and there is little scope for wealth effects.

As indicated, there have been at least two channels through which external influences contributed to the apparent lack of strong and quick effects of restrictive monetary policy on the real economy. First, capital inflows weakened the authorities' leverage on the financial sector; second, changes in export order inflows tended at times to negate the impact of monetary restraint on output. These two undesirable elements were not completely unrelated. Speculative capital inflows, notably in restrictive periods, were at least partly a natural consequence of the undervalued position of the deutschemark. This also enabled German companies to shift their sales from domestic to foreign markets without much difficulty in restrictive periods. The successive revaluations of the deutschemark since 1969 aimed at producing a position of the German currency commensurate with both internal and external equilibrium.

The achievement of fundamental equilibrium in the external balance alone does not, of course, exclude the possibility of "normal" capital flows —motivated by interest differentials arising from differences in monetary conditions at home and abroad—in the future. The German authorities are fully aware of this problem, and have gradually extended the scope of direct exchange controls on residents' borrowing abroad and domestic investment by non-residents. In 1972 they introduced the Cash Deposit Scheme and licensing requirements with respect to the sale of domestic bonds to non-residents. So far these measures have been relatively successful in checking "normal" non-bank capital flows. The Cash Deposit Scheme should also enlarge the authorities' influence on non-bank sectors' borrowing costs. In contrast to the ceiling control on companies' foreign borrowing (which could not significantly affect the *average* cost of borrowing by the non-bank sectors from domestic and foreign sources, insofar as they can borrow abroad at low rates), the Scheme can raise the average cost by freezing a portion of foreign borrowing proceeds and thereby raising the effective interest rates on foreign borrowing.

Apart from the destabilising effect of capital inflows, the impact of restrictive monetary policy actions on financial markets may also have been attenuated by certain characteristics of the German monetary system and the techniques used by the authorities. The Bundesbank's policy of relying on gradual and pervasive changes in financial markets through bank liquidity management, even if applied to a closed economy, can work successfully only when the various factors entering the relationship between bank liquidity and intermediate financial variables are fairly predictable. German experience in this respect suggests that such prediction is not always easy. Possibly in view of this problem, new instruments of monetary policy such as reserve requirements on bank loans and credit ceilings are now under consideration to strengthen the authorities' influence on financial markets. For the moment, the external constraint problem remains the most preoccupying. But, if a solution to the problem of speculative capital flows can be found, and if a greater success is achieved in preventing the re-emergence of fundamental disequilibrium, German monetary policy, with some sharpening of techniques, could become a more effective instrument of demand management.

APPENDICES

Appendix I

BANK LIQUIDITY AND THE FACTORS AFFECTING IT

As indicated in the text, bank "liquidity" consists of those assets (or rights to borrow) which can readily be converted into central bank balances to meet the minimum reserve requirement. Most of the factors affecting liquidity operate in the first instance through changes in a bank's reserve balance itself; if this is reduced (e.g. through an increase in currency in circulation, a balance of payments deficit or a shift of non-bank deposits from commercial banks to the central bank), or needs to be replenished because of an increase in required reserves, banks sell liquid assets to the Bundesbank or draw upon Bundesbank credits. Conversely, if balances at the Bundesbank rise above the required amount, the banks tend to exchange them immediately for interest-bearing liquid assets—or to repay debt to the Bundesbank. This appendix describes in more detail than the main text the various factors affecting bank liquidity; in Appendix II are discussed the various ways in which banks adjust their stock of "liquidity" in response to the changes therein with which they are faced.

A. Policy Factors Affecting Bank Liquidity

Minimum Reserve Requirements

Changes in minimum reserve requirements are the main weapon for affecting bank liquidity. Between mid-1959 and March 1973 this tool has been used 44 times. In some instances, however, these changes applied only to foreign liabilities. Such increases were designed to avoid adding to official exchange reserves, partly as a matter of international monetary co-operation and partly because the additions to bank liquidity resulting from increases in foreign deposits would have been undesirable.

Minimum reserves are held solely in the form of non-interest-bearing deposits with the Bundesbank. The structure of the reserve requirement is complex. It applies, broadly, to all deposits and borrowing with a maturity of less than four years[1] from domestic non-bank sectors and from all non-residents. Certain technical features relating to the base periods used in calculating the requirement make it less stringent than similar require-

---

1. Prior to January 1969, the limitation to maturities of less than four years did not apply to savings deposits. This exception was terminated owing to statistical difficulties of identification; reserve requirements against savings deposits were raised slightly on the termination.

ments in some other countries.[2] There are separate legal maxima for domestic sight liabilities (30 per cent), time liabilities (20 per cent) and savings deposits (10 per cent); bonds issued by banks are exempt.[3] Since August 1969 ratios of up to 100 per cent can be imposed on liabilities to non-residents. Requirements differ between banks in different "reserve classes" (determined by the volume of reserve-carrying liabilities); and depending on whether a bank is situated in a "bank place" (a place where there is a branch office of the Bundesbank). Banks failing to meet the requirement are subject to a penalty interest rate on the shortfall, fixed throughout the period of this study at 3 percentage points over the Lombard rate.

Rediscount Quotas

Access to Bundesbank credit through the discounting of eligible paper has hitherto been virtually automatic within the limits set by the Bundesbank. The unused rediscount margin has therefore been included in the Bundesbank's measure of bank liquidity, and changes in the limits are a policy measure affecting it.

Standard quotas are based on banks' capital (or "own") funds, with somewhat different formulas applicable to different types of banks. The quotas increase automatically with the growth of own funds in the banks' balance sheets, and are recalculated by the authorities each month. But the authorities are free to alter the base of the calculation, to change the quotas upwards or downwards, at any time. These changes usually affect the whole—or at least the greater part—of the banking system. Decreases are more common than increases; the natural growth of balance sheets largely obviates the need for the latter, and requires the former.

Not all cuts in rediscount quotas are determined by the credit policy needs of the moment; but the longer-run need to keep the totals within reasonable limits is always taken into account. From the banks' point of view, cuts in the quotas have the advantage—as compared with increases in minimum reserve ratios—of not reducing their interest-earning assets; but they are nevertheless unwelcome, particularly when liquidity is becoming constricted, because they directly narrow a major route of access to the lender of last resort. For this reason, their use is usually tempered by prior announcement by the Bundesbank, often several months in advance. Thus, the reduction announced in April 1969 became effective in two steps—in July and October. Cuts were regarded as particularly

---

2. Reserve requirements may generally be calculated either:
— on the daily average of liabilities from the 16th of the previous to the 15th of the current month;
— or on the average outstanding on four fixed "bank reporting" days, two in the latter half of the previous month and two in the early half of the current month.
The second method, which was abandoned with respect to foreign sight liabilities in May 1972, would normally give a bank greater freedom in the management of its balances with the Bundesbank. But the Bundesbank may exclude it when it has reason to assume that a bank has taken advantage of it. *Fulfilment* of the requirement is measured by daily average balances at the Bundesbank over the calendar month.
3. For other, minor, exemptions see the Bundesbank's "Order on Minimum Reserves" published in its *Annual Reports*.

heavy blows at bank liquidity. In 1965, half of a cut decided in May, to take effect from October, was postponed because the balance of payments deficit was judged to be constraining bank liquidity sufficiently; as the balance of payments moved into surplus, it was decided in January to make the postponed half of the cut effective in May 1966.

Paper has to meet certain qualifications to be eligible for rediscount. Chiefly it must bear the signatures of at least three parties "known to be solvent" and to have less than 3 months to run on the date of discounting. Certain types of paper eligible for purchase by the Bundesbank under its money market regulations are also eligible for discount. Banks will normally hold sufficient eligible paper to enable them to make full use of their rediscount quotas.

In the absence of published data on the Bundesbank's buying rates for money market paper, the discount rate's relation to these cannot be precisely determined. It is frequently lower than rates on interbank money (see Chart 17 of the main text). Thus, it would seem not to play the role of a "penalty rate". A "high" discount rate does not normally discourage banks from making reasonably full use of their discount quotas, as long as there exists an unsatisfied demand for loans at going interest rates—which are always higher than the discount rate. Before April 1967, there was a formal link between most categories of lending rates and the discount rate.[4] Deposit rates were also adjusted to changes in the discount rate, although not automatically.

Open Market Operations Affecting Bank Liquidity

The bulk of the Bundesbank's open market operations consists of transactions in "liquid" assets with banks; since the Bundesbank always stands ready to repurchase such paper, these operations cannot be used to affect the volume of liquidity. They are discussed, along with other "uses" of bank liquidity, in Appendix II. This section describes only those open market operations—so far of relatively minor importance— that can be used to affect liquidity.

The first of these is transactions in money market paper with non-bank institutions.

BUNDESBANK TRANSACTIONS IN MONEY MARKET PAPER
WITH NON-BANKS[1]
DM billion ; Purchases +, Sales —

1962	+ 0.55	1968	+ 0.16
1963	+ 0.06	1969	— 0.72
1964	+ 0.07	1970	— 2.06
1965	— 0.09	1971	— 0.33
1966	+ 0.01	1972	+ 0.25
1967	0.00		

1. Since 1968 non-banks include the Federal Post Office; formerly the Post Office was treated as a bank, as far as statistics on bank liquidity were concerned.

Source : Deutsche Bundesbank.

4. See Chart 17.

For much of the period under study such transactions were deliberately kept at a relatively low level. Although sales to a wider public could have been used to affect bank liquidity, it was felt that it would be disadvantageous to permit the general public to hold a large volume of easily-monetisable liquid assets, which could lead to a conflict between the needs of credit policy and of the financing of short-term public indebtedness. In addition, the Bundesbank was—as indeed it still is—reluctant to appear in direct competition with the banks by attracting deposits away from them.

Since mid-1971 the Bundesbank has offered short-term open market paper to the general public; it is sold in minimum quantities of DM 5,000 through local branch offices of the Deutsche Bundesbank. Rates have been made competitive with bank deposit rates; they are somewhat higher for a special type of liquidity paper not encashable at the Bundesbank prior to maturity. Also long-term securities have been used, but only on a limited scale. This kind of operation was begun in the latter half of 1967 to stem upward pressures on long-term interest rates resulting from large issues of long-term public sector bonds to finance reflationary budgets. By the second half of 1968 sales predominated, and in early February 1969 the Bundesbank's announcement that it would no longer make purchases on its own account[5] was the first step away from its easy money policies. With three exceptions, since 1969, small sales have been made out of its portfolio each month.

OPEN MARKET TRANSACTIONS IN LONG-TERM SECURITIES
DM billion ; Purchases +, Sales —

1967 second half	+ 1.18
1968 first half	+ 0.04
1968 second half	— 0.32
1969	— 0.50
1970	— 0.23
1971	— 0.06
1972	— 0.10

Source : Deutsche Bundesbank.

Open market policy has been resorted to with some reluctance; the potential disadvantages of open market operations in long-term securities are thought to outweigh the advantages. It has been generally felt that conditions in the capital market should be allowed freely to reflect shifts in the supply of, and demand for, long-term loanable funds—while recognising that monetary policy has a substantial and quick influence on long-term credit markets. In 1967 Bundesbank purchases of long-term securities were undertaken largely because of investors' high liquidity preference. Though the innovation of deficit spending by the public authorities had led to some nervousness—and to the fear that interest rates

5. The main public authority issuers—through the Bundesbank, as their agent—constantly operate in the market to moderate interest rate fluctuations of their own issues. But these transactions do not affect the net supply of bank credit to the economy, and are not recorded in the Bundesbank's balance sheet.

would soon rise again rather sharply, the—publicly announced—large purchases by the Bundesbank soon helped to calm these doubts.

Government Deposits with the Bundesbank

The Federal and Länder governments are required to keep their liquid balances with the Bundesbank, unless the latter gives approval for their investment elsewhere. Thus the movements of such balances are considered to be an "autonomous" factor affecting bank liquidity and are so treated in the statistics. But flexibility in granting approval to deposit balances in other banks can also be used to influence bank liquidity; for example, this was done for short periods in the summer of 1967, when the Bundesbank allowed a certain increase in public authority deposits in the banks. Normally, however, approval is only given where a substantial part of a Land authority's business has traditionally been in the hands of a particular bank.

B. AUTONOMOUS FACTORS AFFECTING BANK LIQUIDITY

There have been large fluctuations in each of the main influences on bank liquidity which are not directly susceptible to monetary policy —external transactions, public authorities' net balances with the Bundesbank, public authorities' money market indebtedness to the banks (other than that arising out of the Bundesbank's money market operations), and the note and coin circulation.

External Transactions

The influence of external transactions on bank liquidity is measured by changes in net foreign reserve assets of the Bundesbank plus the change in those holdings of "short-term balances with foreign banks and investments in foreign money market paper" that may be freely converted into reserve balances at the Bundesbank. Clearly, measurement of this component is difficult. Its definition, and policy measures to influence the distribution of foreign asset accruals between the central bank and the commercial banks, are discussed in Appendix II.

Public Sector Financing

The "autonomous" impact of public sector financing on bank liquidity is measured by two factors: changes in public sector "net balances" at the central bank (discussed in this paragraph) and changes in the banks' holdings of "liquid" public sector securities *other than those arising from open market operations* (discussed in the next paragraph). Net balances are defined by the Bundesbank as the net of balances *with* the Bundesbank minus direct cash advances ("book credits") *by* the Bundesbank. (The effect of changes in Bundesbank holdings of government long-term debt, and of short-term debt resulting from transactions with non-banks, is discussed on pages 15-18 above.) In general, the net balances move in the same direction as the surplus or deficit in the budget. But the movement is substantially dampened by public authorities' borrowing in the capital market or directly from banks—receipts from which are also held with the Bundesbank. As noted above, the Bundesbank can modify the requirement that balances be kept with it, to have a direct policy effect on bank liquidity. But relatively little use appears to have been made of this weapon, and its use cannot be statistically measured.

Bank liquidity is also affected by the issue and redemption of "liquid" securities—bills and bonds—by the public sector. Prior to 1967, however, the effects were slight, reflecting the then relatively small volume of government debt in this form. Practically all of such issues are taken by the banks; to the extent that proceeds are being spent, purchases will increase liquidity in that the paper in question is eligible for purchase by the central bank within the latter's money market operations. Since practically all "liquid" government securities are held by the banking system, increases in the amount of such debt outstanding have the same effect on bank liquidity as reductions in government deposits with the central bank. Thus in 1969, with the public sector in financial surplus, part of the surplus was used to increase balances with (or reduce direct advances from) the Bundesbank, and part was used to redeem short-term government paper held by the banks; the effect on bank liquidity was the same in both cases.

Currency in Circulation

While increases of currency in circulation—including the holdings of banks themselves—constitute a drain on bank liquidity, it tends to vary roughly with changes in nominal income (also in seasonal payment patterns and in declining trends as a proportion of the money supply M_1) and can readily be taken into consideration in formulating monetary policy.

THE COMPONENTS OF BANK LIQUIDITY AND THE FACTORS AFFECTING THEM

As noted in the text, Bundesbank policy designed to influence the disposition of bank liquidity, or the relation between it and the volume of other bank assets, cannot be logically separated from its interest rate policy. This appendix describes both the components of liquidity and, where relevant, the interest rate measures which impinge on them.

In general, banks may dispose of their liquidity in any way they wish. Disposition among the various types of liquid assets will normally be governed by their relative yields or costs, which are largely under the control of the Bundesbank. However, the extent to which Lombard credits may be used is at the Bundesbank's discretion; thus the decision as to whether a reduction in liquidity shall consist of an increase in Lombard credits does not rest on considerations of relative profitability alone.

DOMESTIC MONEY MARKET ASSETS

Domestic money market paper is liquid because the Bundesbank always stands ready to buy it whenever offered, at relatively stable rates. It comprises:

a) Treasury bills (30-90 day maturities);

b) Non-interest-bearing Treasury bonds, i.e. bonds sold at a discount from par (3 months' to 2 years' maturity);

c) Kassenobligationen: interest-bearing notes with 3-4 years' maturity issued by the Federal government, its agencies, and the Länder. Eligibility is restricted to Kassenobligationen issued before 1969 with a remaining life to maturity of 18 months. They were made eligible for the first time in 1967, to improve their marketability and to enable the public authorities to finance their countercyclical expenditures in a way that would not deprive the banking system of liquidity—indeed, would add to it;

d) Storage agency bills (bills issued for the financing of commodity stocks);

e) Prime bankers' acceptances.

The Bundesbank Law requires it to buy and sell paper in the money market "at market prices". In fact, both in its role as the public authorities' agent in transactions in Treasury bills and bonds, and in its attempts to influence the volume of its own transactions with the banks, it sets the market rates itself. Changes in its buying and selling rates are an ancillary weapon of monetary policy, permitting, if desired, finer or more frequent play on the interest rate structure than changes in the discount and Lombard rates. Major changes occur, however, with changes in the discount rate. By changing its rates relative to those prevailing on other forms of bank assets, it can attempt to decelerate or accelerate the expansion of lending to the non-bank sectors, or to divert funds from or to the interbank market. The course of the spectrum of selling rates is shown in Appendix III; the Bundesbank's buying rates are not published but are normally fixed a little above the selling rate by a margin believed to be relatively stable.

The quotation of a rate on money market paper by the Bundesbank does not mean that it is prepared to sell to banks on demand. Generally a rate has been set to guide the marketing of short-term public debt, but the Bundesbank can abstain from selling if it so desires. In October 1969, in an attempt to congeal some part of bank liquidity for a relatively long period, it renewed sales of 18-24 months bonds, after a pause throughout the previous period of cyclical slowing down; in January 1960 it suspended sales of 60-90 day Treasury bills. In the summer of 1967, with large new issues of short-term paper by the public authorities, it generally forbore selling mobilisation paper in order to prevent short-term interest rates from going up. This planning of short-term government debt has reduced sales of such paper to a very low level. The swing to a budget surplus—one of the major factors influencing the total volume of bank liquidity in 1969—resulted mainly in the repayment of government short-term debt held by the banks. At the same time banks reduced their holdings of mobilisation paper almost to zero. More recently, there has been a general decline in banks' holdings of money market paper. Pressures on their liquidity, coupled with high interest rates in foreign short-term money markets, have led to large borrowing at both the discount and Lombard windows, and under such circumstances the banks have naturally preferred to dispose of their lower-yielding money market paper.

FOREIGN LIQUID ASSETS OF COMMERCIAL BANKS

Short-term foreign assets have been a significant component of the total "liquidity" of the banking system. Like domestic open market paper, these assets can be "sold" to the Bundesbank at any time in exchange for reserve deposits.[1] They comprise claims at foreign banks with periods of up to one year (but exclude claims denominated in foreign currencies due at sight, which are regarded as "working balances") and foreign bills of exchange and Treasury bills acquired as money market investments. The definition is somewhat arbitrary and is recognised to be so.[2]

---

1. Automatic intervention was suspended during the period of the floating deutschemark in 1971 and is now (since March 1973) confined to a few currencies within the joint floating block.

2. See *Monthly Report of the Deutsche Bundesbank,* July 1970, p. 29. Apart from the difficulties mentioned there, apparently no allowance is made for the fact that part of the foreign liquid assets included may be the counterpart of liabilities *payable* in foreign currencies, and that therefore banks might be reluctant to convert them into DM balances. The degree of reluctance would presumably depend on relative interest and forward exchange rates.

The central bank has from time to time taken steps to influence directly the amount of bank liquidity held in this form. Usually this has consisted of offering the banks cover ("swaps") at rates which have encouraged the banks to maintain or increase such balances, and withdrawing the offer when it wished to see them reduced. Another device has been to permit banks to offset such balances against foreign-owned deposits in calculating required reserves. Such policies have had, generally, a dual objective—one essentially international, the other domestic. On the international side, they have served to prevent an unwanted increase in official reserves, along with the problem of deciding about reserve composition that such an increase would have presented. But they have also served a domestic monetary objective, similar to that achieved by encouraging the banks to invest in money market paper. Provided with a liquid—in this case foreign—investment at remunerative rates, banks may be discouraged from expanding credits to non-banks or from placing funds in the domestic interbank market.

UNUSED REDISCOUNT QUOTAS

The extent to which discount facilities are available is determined by the authorities, and changes in the availability are a policy factor that affects bank liquidity. But how much of this quota should be used at any particular time and, therefore, how much unused quota remains available, is for the banks to decide. Decisions will depend on, among other things, the income to be gained from earning assets (domestic or foreign, including liquid assets) relative to the cost of obtaining discount credits. Frequently the banks have preferred to increase their use of discount credits rather than reduce their other holdings of liquid assets.

EXCESS BALANCES AT THE CENTRAL BANK

These are ordinarily held in negligible amounts, though from time to time they may rise sharply on a particular day.

LOMBARD CREDITS

In the Bundesbank's estimates of bank liquidity the net liabilities resulting from the use of Lombard credits have been subtracted from the sum of the other components; within the limits permitted by central bank policy, banks can allow reductions in their liquidity to take the form of Lombard borrowing, and increases to take the form of repayment. But since June 1973 the Bundesbank uses a new definition of bank liquidity. Instead of deducting Lombard credit granted, it now includes, as a positive item, the banks' free (or unused) Lombard margin, i.e. the difference at any time between the so-called "warning point"[3] and the Lombard facilities actually used.

The Bundesbank is authorized to grant Lombard credits—like discount credits—for periods of up to three months. The range of eligible instruments is very wide—from commercial bills to long-term bonds. Among

---

3. 20 per cent of the existing total rediscount facilities made available by the Bundesbank.

the latter are included some international issues. It is practically a condition of a bond issue's acceptability by the market that it be of a type eligible as collateral for Lombard credit. No formal ceilings existed on their use until August 1970. The rule was then established that banks' use of Lombard facilities should not exceed 20 per cent of their rediscount quotas.

In practice, the Bundesbank has been much less willing than its scope would allow to grant Lombard credits. Its Credit Policy Regulations[4] state that:

> "The question whether an advance against securities can be granted will be decided according to the general credit situation and the individual circumstances of the would-be borrower. In principle an advance against securities shall be granted only where the object is to cover for a short period a temporary need for liquidity, and where there are no objections to the purpose of the borrowing."

From 1st June 1973 the authorities suspended Lombard facilities until further notice.

BANKS' USE OF DISCOUNT AND LOMBARD CREDITS
DM BILLION ; END OF PERIOD, UNLESS OTHERWISE STATED

	Discount credits	Lombard credits
End-1958 to January 1969		
Minima	0.55 (October 1958)	0.01 (November 1961)
Maxima	20.29 (September 1970)	2.97 (November 1969)
Recent developments		
1969 September	7.75	0.04
October	8.92	1.23
November	11.93	2.97
December	14.86	2.80
(7th December)	(13.71)	(5.08)
1970 March	19.35	2.68
June	19.45	0.82
September	20.29	1.17
December	17.06	1.68
1971 March	17.28	1.12
June	19.65	0.38
September	2.31	2.36
December	17.41	1.40
1972 March	18.97	0.55
June	16.36	0.10
September	19.14	2.23
December	19.03	1.15
1973 January	18.00	1.32

Source : Deutsche Bundesbank.

4. Credit Policy Regulation, Bundesbank *Annual Report* for 1968, p. 108.

Throughout most of the period under review, the interest rate on Lombard credits was one per cent above the discount rate (Chart 17 of the main text). In early September 1969, a brief experiment was made with a scale of rates (from 6 to 8 per cent), depending on a bank's borrowing in relation to its capital and reserves. Although the experiment was not continued, the gap between the discount and Lombard rates has been kept wider than previously. Immediately after the revaluation, it was hoped that the change in parity would soon have a sufficiently dampening effect on economic activity to allow a general reduction in interest rates. While the Lombard rate was raised to have an immediate effect on banks' borrowing from the Bundesbank, the discount rate was kept stable because no general pressure on rates was desired. In any event, the use of Lombard credit rose very sharply. This reflected partly the near exhaustion of rediscount quotas by a number of banks; partly the substantial profit to be gained around the turn of the year by borrowing at the Lombard window and placing the funds in short-term investments abroad. With the changes in December 1969, the gap between the discount and Lombard rates was widened to 3 per cent. But during the period up to October 1971 it was gradually narrowed again to a one per cent differential.

Since October-November 1972, when the Lombard rate was raised to 2 per cent over the discount rate, the Bundesbank has returned to its earlier practice of widening the gap between its lending rates. This has mainly been provoked by the regularly extensive use of Lombard credit by the banking system since 1969.

Appendix III

CHRONOLOGY OF PRINCIPAL MONETARY MEASURES

1959

SEPTEMBER

Discount rate	Raised from 2.75 to 3.00 per cent.
Lombard rate	Raised from 3.75 to 4.00 per cent.
Money market selling rates	Raised—in three successive steps—by a total of 0.75 per cent.

OCTOBER

Discount rate	Raised from 3.00 to 4.00 per cent.
Lombard rate	Raised from 4.00 to 5.00 per cent.
Money market selling rates	Raised over the month as a whole by 0.875-1.00 percentage points. Renewal of sales of mobilisation paper with maturities of 18 and 24 months.
Rediscount quotas	As a measure of basic reform, lowered by almost 20 per cent.

NOVEMBER

Minimum reserve ratios .	Increased by 10 per cent on all domestic and foreign liabilities.

DECEMBER

Money market selling rates	Raised by 0.125 percentage points

1960

JANUARY

Minimum reserve ratios .	Raised:
	— by a further 10 per cent on domestic and

foreign liabilities incurred before 30th November 1959;

— to the legal maxima on foreign liabilities incurred after 30th November 1959.

FEBRUARY

Money market selling rates   Raised on all maturities by 0.125 percentage points.

MARCH

Minimum reserve ratios .   Raised by 20 per cent.

Rediscount quotas . . . . . .   Lowered as a *credit policy* measure by 10 per cent of the first DM 5 million available to any one bank, and by 30 per cent of the remainder. Effect substantially greater than that of increase in minimum reserve ratios.

Money market selling rates   Raised on all maturities by 0.125 percentage points.

JUNE

Discount rate . . . .   Raised from 4.00 to 5.00 per cent.

Lombard rate . . . .   Raised from 5.00 to 6.00 per cent.

Money market selling rates   Raised by 0.75-0.875 percentage points.

Minimum reserve ratios .   Raised by 15 per cent on sight and time liabilities and by 10 per cent on savings deposits. Suspension of provision for the "offsetting" of banks' short-term foreign assets in the calculation of minimum reserve requirements on foreign liabilities.

Other measures against capital inflows . . . . . .   Interest banned on banks' sight and time foreign deposit liabilities. Banks forbidden to stand security for customers' foreign borrowing. Deposits resulting from customers' drawing on foreign third-party credits in excess of end-May level subjected to maximum legal reserve requirements.

JULY

Minimum reserve ratios .   Raised to the legal maxima on domestic liabilities in excess of the average level during March-May.

Rediscount quotas . . . . .   Lowered as a *credit policy* measure by 5 per cent of the first DM 5 million available to any one bank; and by 10 per cent of the remainder. With cut in March, a cumulative lowering of 15 per cent on the first

114

DM 5 million; and of 40 per cent on the remainder. Cuts in *total* quotas since September estimated at about one-third; reduction in *unused* quotas over the same period about one-half.

AUGUST

Money market regulation .	Bank members of the Federal Loan Syndicate agree to take up DM 1 billion of *non-negotiable* mobilisation paper, with maturity of two years. Not returnable to Bundesbank except in cases of emergency. Yield of $5\frac{1}{2}$ per cent (the current rate offered by the Bundesbank on *negotiable* paper).

NOVEMBER

Discount rate	Lowered from 5.00 to 4.00 per cent.
Lombard rate	Lowered from 6.00 to 5.00 per cent.
Money market selling rates	Lowered by 0.875 percentage points.

DECEMBER

Minimum reserve ratios .	Termination of special ratios on incremental domestic liabilities.
Money market selling rates	Lowered by 0.25 percentage points.

1961

JANUARY

Discount rate	Lowered from 4.00 to 3.50 per cent.
Lombard rate	Lowered from 5.00 to 4.50 per cent.
Money market selling rates	Lowered by 0.5 percentage points.

FEBRUARY

Minimum reserve ratios .	Lowered by 5 per cent on all domestic liabilities.
Money market selling rates	Lowered by 0.25 percentage points.
Forward exchange rate ..	Premium initially reduced from 1 to $\frac{1}{2}$ per cent and finally terminated.
Rediscount quotas	Partial rescission of previous cuts.

MARCH

Minimum reserve ratios ..	Lowered in two steps of 5 per cent each on all domestic liabilities.

Money market selling rates	Lowered by 0.5 percentage points.
Exchange rate	DEUTSCHEMARK REVALUED by 5 per cent to a new parity of DM 4.0 per U.S. dollar.

APRIL

Minimum reserve ratios .	Lowered by 5 per cent on all domestic liabilities.
Money market selling rates	Lowered by 0.125 percentage points.

MAY

Discount rate	Lowered from 3.50 to 3.00 per cent.
Lombard rate	Lowered from 4.50 to 4.00 per cent.
Minimum reserve ratios .	Raised to legal maxima on all foreign liabilities but provision reactivated for the "offsetting" of foreign money market investments. Net effect of easing.
Money market selling rates	Lowered by 0.125 percentage points on all maturities.

JUNE

Minimum reserve ratios .	Lowered by 10 per cent on all domestic liabilities.

JULY

Minimum reserve ratios .	Lowered by 5 per cent on all domestic liabilities.

AUGUST

Minimum reserve ratios .	Lowered by 5 per cent on all domestic liabilities.
Money market regulation .	DM 1 billion sold in non-negotiable form in 3rd quarter 1960 now made eligible for resale to Bundesbank.

SEPTEMBER

Minimum reserve ratios .	Lowered by 5 per cent on all domestic liabilities.
Government deposits ...	DM 760 million of proceeds of Volkswagen sale released under Bundesbank Law, Article 17.

OCTOBER

Minimum reserve ratios .	Lowered by 5 per cent on all domestic liabilities.

Money market selling rates	Lowered by 0.25-0.125 percentage points.

NOVEMBER

Rediscount quotas	Restored fully to levels established in October 1959.

DECEMBER

Minimum reserve ratios .	Lowered by 5 per cent on all domestic liabilities.

1962

JANUARY

Money market selling rates	Lowered by 0.125 percentage points on up to 12 months paper.

FEBRUARY

Minimum reserve ratios .	Special ratios on foreign liabilities eliminated.

MARCH

Money market selling rates	Raised by 0.125 percentage points.

APRIL

Money market selling rates	Raised by 0.125 percentage points.

JUNE

Money market selling rates	Raised by 0.125 percentage points.

JULY

Money market selling rates	Raised by 0.125 percentage points.

AUGUST

Money market selling rates	Raised by 0.125 percentage points.

OCTOBER

Money market selling rates	Raised by 0.125 percentage points.

1963

NOVEMBER

Money market selling rates	Lowered on 18 and 24 months paper by 0.125 percentage points.

1964

March

Measures against capital flows ....

Ban on interest payments on foreign demand deposits extended to foreign time deposits.

Intention to impose *Withholding Tax* announced.

April

Minimum reserve ratios .

Raised to the legal maxima on all foreign deposit liabilities.

August

Minimum reserve ratios .

Raised by 10 per cent on all domestic liabilities.

September

Rediscount quotas .....

Lowered by the amount of a bank's borrowing from abroad in excess of the average outstanding 31st January-30th June 1964. Transactions to finance imports and entrepot trade excluded.

December

Lombard rate ....

Reduced by 0.75 percentage points on advances taken between 10th-31st December *only*.

1965

January

Discount rate .... — Raised from 3.00 to 3.50 per cent.

Lombard rate .... — Raised from 4.00 to 4.50 per cent.

Money market selling rates — Raised by 0.5, 0.625 or 0.75 percentage points.

March

Withholding Tax ...... Becomes effective.

May

Rediscount quotas ..... Reduction decided primarily as a regulatory measure, with effect from October.

AUGUST

Discount rate	Raised from 3.50 to 4.00 per cent.
Lombard rate	Raised from 4.50 to 5.00 per cent.
Rate on cash advances ..	Raised from 3.50 to 4.00 per cent.
Money market selling rates	Raised by 0.625 or 0.75 percentage points.
Rediscount quotas	Cut scheduled for October (see May 1965) reduced by half; remainder postponed indefinitely.

OCTOBER

Rediscount quotas	Cut by about DM 1.3 billion (see May and August 1965).

DECEMBER

Minimum reserve ratios .	For December only, reduced by about 9 per cent against sight and time liabilities to residents.

1966

JANUARY

Rediscount quotas	Decision to make postponed cut (see May, August and October 1965) effective May 1966.
Money market selling rates	Raised by 0.125 or 0.5 percentage points.

FEBRUARY

Money market selling rates	Raised by 0.125 percentage points on paper of six months and over.

MARCH

Money market selling rates	Raised by 0.125 percentage points on paper of six months and over.

MAY

Discount rate	Raised from 4.00 to 5.00 per cent.
Lombard rate	Raised from 5.00 to 6.25 per cent.
Money market selling rates	Raised by 0.50 or 1 percentage point.

DECEMBER

Minimum reserve ratios .	Lowered (initially for December only) by about 9 per cent on resident sight and time liabilities.
Money market selling rates	Lowered by 0.25 percentage points.

119

1967

JANUARY

Discount rate	Lowered from 5.00 to 4.50 per cent.
Lombard rate	Lowered from 6.25 to 5.50 per cent.
Money market selling rates	Lowered—in several steps—by 0.625 percentage points.
Minimum reserve ratios .	Prolongation of reduction originally decided for December only.
	Suspension of provision for the "offsetting" of banks' foreign short-term investments in calculating minimum reserve requirements.

FEBRUARY

Discount rate	Lowered from 4.50 to 4.00 per cent.
Lombard rate	Lowered from 5.50 to 5.00 per cent.
Money market selling rates	Lowered by 0.375 percentage points.
Minimum reserve ratios .	On all foreign liabilities, reduced to the ratios on equivalent domestic liabilities.

MARCH

Minimum reserve ratios .	On all liabilities, reduced by 10 per cent.

APRIL

Discount rate	Lowered from 4.00 to 3.50 per cent.
Lombard rate	Lowered from 5.00 to 4.50 per cent.
Money market selling rates	Lowered by between 0.125 and 0.5 percentage points.
Interest rates	Repeal of Interest Rates Order.

MAY

Discount rate	Lowered from 3.50 to 3.00 per cent.
Lombard rate	Lowered from 4.50 to 4.00 per cent.
Minimum reserve ratios .	On all liabilities, reduced by 10 per cent.
Money market selling rates	Lowered by 0.375 or 0.50 percentage points.

JUNE

Money market selling rates	Lowered on up to 90 days paper by 0.25 percentage points.
Money market regulation .	Inclusion of Länder non-interest bearing Treasury bonds up to an amount of DM 1.2 billion within the Bundesbank's money market regulation.

| Law for the Promotion of Stability and Growth .. | Becomes effective. |

JULY

| Minimum reserve ratios . | Lowered on all liabilities by about 8 per cent. |

AUGUST

Minimum reserve ratios .	Lowered on all liabilities by about 6 per cent.
Lombard rate	Lowered from 4.00 to 3.50 per cent.
Open market operations in long-term securities ..	Started in support of public authorities' loan issues.
Money market regulation .	Inclusion of Kassenobligationen (medium-term notes) of Federal government, Railways and Postal Administration with remaining life of up to 18 months within the Bundesbank's money market regulation.

SEPTEMBER

| Minimum reserve ratios . | Lowered:
— on savings deposits by about 11 per cent;
— on other liabilities by about 2.5 per cent. |

OCTOBER

| Money market regulation . | Inclusion of Kassenobligationen of the Länder with remaining life of up to 18 months within the Bundesbank's money market regulation. |

1968

DECEMBER

| Minimum reserve ratios . | Raised to 100 per cent on increments to foreign liabilities above the level of 15th November. |
| Other measures to restrain capital inflows ...... | Banks required to obtain authorisation for the acceptance of foreign funds, except in connection with "normal" current and capital transactions. |

1969

FEBRUARY

| Minimum reserve ratios . | Base date for calculation of 100 per cent reserve requirement on incremental foreign |

121

liabilities now made optionally 15th November or 15th January; other minor easements in the calculation of the requirement.

Open market operations in long-term securities ..	Terminated.

MARCH

Lombard rate	Raised from 3.50 to 4.00 per cent.
Rediscount quotas	20 per cent reduction decided, to be fully effective by July.

APRIL

Minimum reserve ratios .	100 per cent ratio against foreign liabilities retained with base date brought forward to 15th or 30th April 1969.
Discount rate	Raised from 3.00 to 4.00 per cent.
Lombard rate	Raised from 4.00 to 5.00 per cent.
Money market selling rates	Raised by between 0.625 and 1 percentage point.

JUNE

Discount rate	Raised from 4.00 to 5.00 per cent.
Lombard rate	Raised from 5.00 to 6.00 per cent.
Money market selling rates	Raised by 0.75 or 1 percentage point.
Minimum reserve ratios .	Raised by about 15 per cent against domestic liabilities and by 50 per cent against those foreign liabilities not already subject to 100 per cent requirements.

JULY

Rediscount quotas	See March 1969.

AUGUST

Minimum reserve ratios .	Raised by about 10 per cent against all liabilities (except foreign liabilities already subject to 100 per cent requirements).

SEPTEMBER

Lombard rate	Temporary penalty rates of 7 per cent imposed from 1st-10th September, if use of Lombard credit exceeded twice a bank's capital and reserves; and of 8 per cent, if it exceeded them fourfold.

122

Exchange rate	DEUTSCHEMARK ALLOWED TO FLOAT.
Discount rate	Raised from 5.00 to 6.00 per cent.
Lombard rate	Raised from 6.00 to 7.50 per cent.
Money market selling rates	Raised by 0.75 or 1 percentage point.

OCTOBER

Exchange rate	DEUTSCHEMARK REVALUED by 9.3 per cent to a new parity of DM 3.66 per U.S. dollar.

NOVEMBER

Minimum reserve ratios .	Abolition of 100 per cent reserve requirement on incremental foreign liabilities; all special ratios against foreign liabilities abolished; and reserve requirements generally reduced by 10 per cent.

DECEMBER

Lombard rate	Raised from 7.50 to 9.00 per cent.
Minimum reserve ratios .	Reduced by 10 per cent for December only.
Money market selling rates	Raised by between 0.125 and 0.375 percentage points.

1970

MARCH

Discount rate	Raised from 6.00 to 7.50 per cent.
Lombard rate	Raised from 9.00 to 9.50 per cent.
Money market selling rates	Raised by between 0.75 and 1.50 percentage points.
Minimum reserve ratios .	Supplementary 30 per cent ratio imposed on increments to foreign liabilities above the level of the four-weekly average level of February or of the level of 6th March.

JULY

Discount rate	Reduced from 7.50 to 7.00 per cent.
Lombard rate	Reduced from 9.50 to 9.00 per cent.
Money market selling rates	Reduced by 0.25 percentage points on maturities up to 90 days.

JULY

Minimum reserve ratios .	Raised by 15 per cent.

September

Minimum reserve ratios .	Supplementary ratios (40 per cent on sight and time deposits, 20 per cent on savings deposits) imposed on additions to liabilities above the April-June average, subject to the condition that the ratios on all liabilities should not exceed the legal maxima. Special ratios on foreign liabilities abolished.

November

Discount rate	Reduced from 7.00 to 6.50 per cent.
Lombard rate	Reduced from 9.00 to 8.00 per cent.
Minimum reserve ratios .	Supplementary ratio abolished on increase in domestic liabilities. Basic reserves on all liabilities raised by 15 per cent. Supplemental reserve of 30 per cent on external liabilities above the average of 23rd and 31st October and 7th and 15th November.

December

Discount rate	Reduced from 6.50 to 6.00 per cent.
Lombard rate	Reduced from 8.00 to 7.50 per cent.

1971

April

Discount rate	Reduced from 6.00 to 5.00 per cent.
Lombard rate	Reduced from 7.50 to 6.50 per cent.
Rediscount quotas	Reduced by 10 per cent.
Open market operations .	Transactions with non-banks "intensified".
Money market selling rates	Reduced by 1 percentage point on maturities up to 90 days.

May

Exchange rate	DEUTSCHEMARK ALLOWED TO FLOAT.
Open market operations .	Further intensified. Discountable Treasury bonds now also sold to non-bank public.

June

Minimum reserve ratios .	Raised by 15 per cent on domestic liabilities. The ratio on foreign liabilities raised to a level twice as high as the *new* domestic ratio.
Money market selling rates	Reduced by 0.5 percentage points on maturities up to 90 days.

OCTOBER

Discount rate	Reduced from 5.00 to 4.50 per cent.
Lombard rate	Reduced from 6.50 to 5.50 per cent.
Money market selling rates	Reduced by 0.5 percentage points for maturities up to 90 days.
Supplementary rediscount for third-country bills .	Abolished.

NOVEMBER

Minimum reserve ratios .	Reduced by 10 per cent on domestic liabilities.

DECEMBER

Discount rate	Reduced from 4.50 to 4.00 per cent.
Lombard rate	Reduced from 5.50 to 5.00 per cent.
Money market selling rates	Reduced by 0.5 percentage points on maturities up to 90 days.
Exchange rate	Following the Washington conference on exchange rate relationships (Washington, 17th-18th December), the "Central rate" (Leitkurs) for the deutschemark is temporarily fixed at DM 3.2225 per U.S. dollar with effect from 21st December. This represents a revaluation of 13.6 per cent from the earlier dollar parity.

1972

JANUARY

Minimum reserve ratios .	Reduced by 10 per cent on domestic liabilities.

FEBRUARY

Discount rate	Reduced from 4.00 to 3.00 per cent.
Lombard rate	Reduced from 5.00 to 4.00 per cent.
Money market selling rates	Reduced by 0.5 percentage points on maturities up to 90 days.

MARCH

Cash deposits requirement	Introduced on certain types of borrowing from abroad, particularly by non-banks. Ratio fixed at 40 per cent of the liabilities subject to this requirement. Deposits held interest-free at the Bundesbank.

JUNE

Sales of bonds to non-residents	Restricted; mandatory authorisation introduced.

JULY

Minimum reserve ratios .	Raised by 20 per cent on domestic liabilities, and from 31.7 to 40 per cent, 22 to 35 per cent and 16.2 to 30 per cent on basic requirements against non-resident sight, time, and savings deposits. The incremental requirement on non-residents' deposits raised from 40 to 60 per cent.
Rediscount quotas	Reduced by 10 per cent.
Cash deposit ratio	Raised by 25 per cent to 50 per cent. Also substantial reduction in the maximum amount of borrowing exempted from cash deposit requirements; notification of "sales" of foreign claims now mandatory.

AUGUST

Minimum reserve ratios .	Raised by 10 per cent on domestic liabilities.
Rediscount quotas	Reduced by 10 per cent.

OCTOBER

Discount rate	Raised from 3.00 to 3.50 per cent.
Lombard rate	Raised from 4.00 to 5.00 per cent.
Money market selling rates	Raised by 0.5 percentage points on maturities up to 90 days.

NOVEMBER

Discount rate	Raised from 3.50 to 4.00 per cent.
Lombard rate	Raised from 5.00 to 6.00 per cent.
Money market selling rates	Raised by 0.5 percentage points on maturities up to 90 days.
Open market operations .	Stimulated, particularly with respect to non-banks. The rates for discountable Treasury bonds not included in the money market regulating arrangements (non-returnable before maturity) raised by 0.75 per cent.

DECEMBER

Discount rate	Raised from 4.00 to 4.50 per cent.
Lombard rate	Raised from 6.00 to 6.50 per cent.
Money market selling rates	Raised by 0.5 percentage points on maturities up to 90 days.

JANUARY

Discount rate	Raised from 4.50 to 5.00 per cent.
Lombard rate	Raised from 6.50 to 7.00 per cent.
Money market selling rates	Raised by 0.5 percentage points on maturities up to 90 days.
Open market sales of "Bundesbank Notes" to resident non-banks ...	Intensified.
Allowance against cash deposit requirements .	Reduced from DM 500,000 to DM 50,000.

FEBRUARY

Rediscount quotas	Cut by 10 per cent and their use limited to 60 per cent of new total.
Cash deposit requirements	Tightened; the Bundesbank authorised to freeze up to 100 per cent of the growth in foreign liabilities.

MARCH

Minimum reserve requirements	Raised by 15 per cent on domestic sight and time deposits and 7.5 per cent on saving deposits.
$8\frac{1}{2}$ per cent 8-year non-callable stabilisation bonds	Offered for public subscription; the proceeds to be frozen at the Bundesbank.
Exchange rate	DEUTSCHEMARK REVALUED by 3 per cent. The new central rate (expressed for the first time in terms of SDRs): SDR 0.294389.
Access to Lombard credit	Temporarily improved (arrangement terminated on 12th April).

APRIL

Rediscount quotas	Cut by 10 per cent.
Open market operations .	Bills purchased from the banks for a fixed period of ten days; rate set at 12 per cent (arrangement in force between 12th-30th April).

MAY

Discount rate	Raised from 5.00 to 6.00 per cent.

Lombard rate	Raised from 7.00 to 8.00 per cent.
Money market selling rates	Raised by 1 percentage point on maturities up to 90 days.

JUNE

Exchange rate	DEUTSCHEMARK REVALUED by 5.5 per cent. The new central rate: SDR 0.310580.
Discount rate	Raised from 6.00 to 7.00 per cent.
Lombard rate	Raised from 8.00 to 9.00 per cent.
Lombard credits to banks and credit institutions .	Suspended.
Open market operations .	7th June, bills purchased from the banks for a fixed period of 10 days; rate set at 13 per cent. 27th June, rates on money market paper raised by 0.375 per cent.
Entreprises' access to DM-denominated credit within the "free export quota"	Closed.

JULY

The computing base for incremental reserve requirements on foreign liabilities	Reduced by 25 per cent; the measure estimated to increase the banks' deposits at the Bundesbank by DM 1.5 billion.
10 per cent 8-year non-callable stabilisation bonds	Offered for public subscription; redemption possible after 5 years; proceeds to be frozen at the Bundesbank.
General open market operations	Intensified. 24th July, bills are offered for sale to the money market for a fixed period of 10 days at a rate of 15 per cent; offer withdrawn 31st July.

AUGUST

Open market operations .	2nd August, bills offered for sale to the money market for a fixed period of 10 days at a rate of 13 per cent. Resort to "more flexible measures within the open market policy"

announced, with the aim of reducing interest rate fluctuations in the money market; 13th August, offer to sell to banks money market paper at 7 per cent for a period of 10 days; 15th August, additional offer of paper at 6.75 per cent for 5 days.

OECD

Monetary Studies Series

Also available:

MONETARY POLICY IN JAPAN

This report, the first in the series, gives a detailed analysis of the use of monetary policy in Japan during the past decade. The main factor motivating monetary policy—although domestic considerations were also important—was the need to protect the low level of foreign exchange reserves from overly fast domestic expansion or a weakening of demand in Japanese export markets. In this respect, the report on Japan provides much clearer evidence, than those on the other countries under study, of a significant and relatively quick impact of monetary policy on private fixed and inventory investment and, thereby, on domestic output and the trade balance.

December 1972.

108 pages, $ 3.50   £ 1.14   F. 14   Fr. S. 11.10   DM 8.80

MONETARY POLICY IN ITALY

This report, the second in the series, analyses the role of Italian monetary policy in domestic demand management and balance of payments adjustment. The report shows that Italian experience provides a good illustration of the general proposition that, in an open economy with a fixed exchange rate, monetary policy is more effective in achieving the external policy objective than in influencing domestic policy objectives, provided speculation in exchange markets is not important.

May 1973.

92 pages, $ 3.75   £ 1.32   F. 15   Fr. S. 11.90   DM 9.40

Forthcoming:

MONETARY POLICY IN THE UNITED STATES

OECD SALES AGENTS
DEPOSITAIRES DES PUBLICATIONS DE L'OCDE

AUSTRALIA – AUSTRALIE
B.C.N. Agencies Pty, Ltd.,
178 Collins Street, MELBOURNE 3000.
☎ 63.4144
658 Pittwater Road, Brookvale, SYDNEY 2100.

AUSTRIA – AUTRICHE
Gerold and Co., Graben 31, WIEN 1.
☎ 52.22.35

BELGIUM – BELGIQUE
Librairie des Sciences
Coudenberg 76-78, B 1000 BRUXELLES 1.
☎ 13.37.36/12.05.60

BRAZIL — BRESIL
Mestre Jou S.A., Rua Guaipá 518,
Caixa Postal 24090, 05000 SAO PAULO 10.
☎ 256-2746/262-1609
Rua Senador Dantas 19 s/205-6, RIO DE
JANEIRO GB. ☎ 232-07.32

CANADA
Information Canada
171 Slater, OTTAWA. KIA 0S9.
☎ (613) 992-9738

DENMARK – DANEMARK
Munksgaards Boghandel
Nørregade 6, 1165 KØBENHAVN K.
☎ (01) 12 69 70

FINLAND – FINLANDE
Akateeminen Kirjakauppa
Keskuskatu 1, 00100 HELSINKI 10. ☎ 625.901

FRANCE
Bureau des Publications de l'OCDE
2 rue André-Pascal, 75775 PARIS CEDEX 16
☎ 524.81.67
Principaux correspondants :
PARIS : Presses Universitaires de France,
49 bd St-Michel, 75005 Paris. ☎ 325.83.40
Sciences Politiques (Lib.)
30 rue St-Guillaume, 75007 Paris. ☎ 548.36.02
13602 AIX-EN-PROVENCE : Librairie de
l'Université. ☎ 26.18.08
38000 GRENOBLE : B. Arthaud. ☎ 87.25.11
31000 TOULOUSE : Privat. ☎ 21.09.26

GERMANY – ALLEMAGNE
Deutscher Bundes-Verlag G.m.b.H.
Postfach 9380, 53 BONN. ☎ (02221) 233.138
un in den massgebenden Buch handlungen
Deutschlands.

GREECE – GRECE
Librairie Kauffmann, 28 rue du Stade,
ATHENES 132. ☎ 322.21.60

ICELAND – ISLANDE
Snaebjörn Jonsson and Co., h.f.,
Hafnarstræti 4 and 9, P.O.B. 1131,
REYKJAVIK. ☎ 13133/14281/11936

INDIA – INDE
Oxford Book and Stationery Co.:
NEW DELHI, Scindia House. ☎ 47388
CALCUTTA, 17 Park Street. ☎ 24083

IRELAND – IRLANDE
Eason and Son, 40 Lower O'Connell Street,
P.O.B. 42, DUBLIN 1. ☎ 01-41161

ISRAEL
Emanuel Brown :
35 Allenby Road, TEL AVIV. ☎ 51049/54082
also at :
9, Shlomzion Hamalka Street, JERUSALEM.
☎ 234807
48 Nahlath Benjamin Street, TEL AVIV.
☎ 53276

ITALY – ITALIE
Libreria Commissionaria Sansoni :
Via Lamarmora 45, 50121 FIRENZE. ☎ 579751
Via Bartolini 29, 20155 MILANO. ☎ 365083
Sous-dépositaires :
Editrice e Libreria Herder,
Piazza Montecitorio 120, 00186 ROMA.
☎ 674628
Libreria Hoepli, Via Hoepli 5, 20121 MILANO.
☎ 865446
Libreria Lattes, Via Garibaldi 3, 10122 TORINO.
☎ 519274
La diffusione delle edizioni OCDE è inoltre assicu-
rata delle migliori librerie nelle città più importanti.

JAPAN – JAPON
OECD Publications Centre,
Akasaka Park Building,
2-3-4 Akasaka,
Minato-ku
TOKYO 107. ☎ 586-2016
Maruzen Company Ltd.,
6 Tori-Nichome Nihonbashi, TOKYO 103,
P.O.B. 5050, Tokyo International 100-31.
☎ 272-7211

LEBANON – LIBAN
Documenta Scientifica/Redico
Edison Building, Bliss Street,
P.O.Box 5641, BEIRUT, ☎ 354429 – 344425

THE NETHERLANDS – PAYS-BAS
W.P. Van Stockum
Buitenhof 36, DEN HAAG. ☎ 070-65.68.08

NEW ZEALAND – NOUVELLE-ZELANDE
The Publications Officer
Government Printing Office
Mulgrave Street (Private Bag)
WELLINGTON. ☎ 46.807
and Government Bookshops at
AUCKLAND (P.O.B. 5344). ☎ 32.919
CHRISTCHURCH (P.O.B. 1721). ☎ 50.331
HAMILTON (P.O.B. 857). ☎ 80.103
DUNEDIN (P.O.B. 1104) ☎ 78.294

NORWAY – NORVEGE
Johan Grundt Tanums Bokhandel,
Karl Johansgate 41/43, OSLO 1. ☎ 02-332980

PAKISTAN
Mirza Book Agency, 65 Shahrah Quaid-E-Azam,
LAHORE 3. ☎ 66839

PORTUGAL
Livraria Portugal,
Rua do Carmo 70-74. LISBOA 2. ☎ 360582/3

SPAIN – ESPAGNE
Libreria Mundi Prensa
Castelló 37, MADRID-1. ☎ 275.46.55
Libreria Bastinos
Pelayo, 52, BARCELONA 1. ☎ 222.06.00

SWEDEN – SUEDE
Fritzes Kungl. Hovbokhandel,
Fredsgatan 2, 11152 STOCKHOLM 16.
☎ 08/23 89 00

SWITZERLAND – SUISSE
Librairie Payot, 6 rue Grenus, 1211 GENEVE 11
☎ 022-31.89.50
et à LAUSANNE, NEUCHATEL, VEVEY,
MONTREUX, BERNE, BALE, ZURICH.

TAIWAN
Books and Scientific Supplies Services, Ltd.
P.O.B. 83, TAIPEI.

TURKEY – TURQUIE
Librairie Hachette,
469 Istiklal Caddesi,
Beyoglu, ISTANBUL, ☎ 44.94.70
et 14 E Ziya Gökalp Caddesi
ANKARA. ☎ 12.10.80

UNITED KINGDOM – ROYAUME-UNI
H.M. Stationery Office, P.O.B. 569, LONDON
SE1 9 NH
or
49 High Holborn
LONDON WC1V 6HB (personal callers)
Branches at: EDINBURGH, BIRMINGHAM,
BRISTOL, MANCHESTER, CARDIFF,
BELFAST.

UNITED STATES OF AMERICA
OECD Publications Center, Suite 1207,
1750 Pennsylvania Ave, N.W.
WASHINGTON, D.C. 20006. ☎ (202)298-8755

VENEZUELA
Libreria del Este, Avda. F. Miranda 52,
Edificio Galipán, Aptdo. 60 337, CARACAS 106.
☎ 32 23 01/33 26 04/33 24 73

YUGOSLAVIA – YOUGOSLAVIE
Jugoslovenska Knjiga, Terazije 27, P.O.B. 36,
BEOGRAD. ☎ 621-992

Les commandes provenant de pays où l'OCDE n'a pas encore désigné de dépositaire
peuvent être adressées à :
OCDE, Bureau des Publications, 2 rue André-Pascal, 75775 Paris CEDEX 16
Orders and inquiries from countries where sales agents have not yet been appointed may be sent to
OECD, Publications Office, 2 rue André-Pascal, 75775 Paris CEDEX 16

OECD   PUBLICATIONS
2, rue André-Pascal
75775 PARIS CEDEX 16
No. 32,437.   1973.

●

PRINTED IN FRANCE